CANADA AT BRITAIN'S SIDE

Photo by Karsh, Ottawa

CANADA
AT BRITAIN'S SIDE

BY

The Right Honourable

W. L. MACKENZIE KING, M.P.

LONDON
MACMILLAN AND CO., LTD
1941

E000088451

940-671

67239

Copyright, Canada, 1941
By
THE MACMILLAN COMPANY OF CANADA LIMITED

m 1710
940·5371

PRINTED IN CANADA
T. H BEST PRINTING CO., LIMITED
TORONTO, ONT.

WE BELIEVE that everything which free men value and cherish, on this side of the grave, is in peril in this war. The right of men, rich and poor, to be treated as men; the right of men to make the laws by which they shall be governed; the right of men to work where they will at what they will; the right of womankind to the serenity and sanctity of the home; the right of children to play in safety under peaceful heavens; the right of old men and women to the tranquillity of their sunset; the right to speak the truth in our hearts; the right to worship in our own way, the God in whom we believe.

W. L. MACKENZIE KING

This book contains a collection of significant speeches and addresses delivered since the outbreak of war by the Right Honourable W. L. Mackenzie King. They constitute an authoritative account of Canada's part in the war by the Prime Minister of Canada.

In the selections made, the publishers have sought to provide a connected and continuous account of Canada's war effort appropriately set against the background of the struggle itself. As a means of uniting the whole, the selections are preceded by brief notes which give the setting and other relevant facts. The exact texts have been used. Editing has been confined to the deletion of passages which are repetitive or of lesser interest. Where there have been deletions, slight verbal amendments have been made to preserve continuity.

Canada entered the war as a free and united nation at the side of Britain. Mr. Mackenzie King loses no opportunity of emphasizing the determination of the Canadian people to put forth their utmost effort till the hour of victory, and to remain to the end, freely and unitedly, at Britain's side.

THE PUBLISHERS.

CONTENTS

ix

AT BRITAIN'S SIDE

The armed forces of Germany attacked Poland in the early morning of Friday, September 1, 1939. That same day, the Canadian Parliament was summoned to meet in special session on September 7. The Prime Minister announced that the War Measures Act was being invoked and that, in the event of Britain being drawn into war to resist aggression, it was the intention of the government to recommend to parliament that Canada should take up arms at the side of Britain.

On the morning of Sunday, September 3, His Majesty the King proclaimed a state of war between the United Kingdom and Germany. That afternoon the Prime Minister made the following broadcast to the Canadian people.

AT BRITAIN'S SIDE

BROADCAST, SEPTEMBER 3, 1939

U NHAPPILY for the world, Herr Hitler and the Nazi regime in Germany have persisted in the attempt to extend their control over other peoples and countries. They have pursued aggressive designs in wanton disregard of all treaty obligations and peaceful methods of adjusting international disputes. They have had resort increasingly to agencies of deception, terrorism, and violence. It is this reliance upon force, this lust for conquest, this determination to dominate throughout the world, which is the real cause of the war that to-day threatens the freedom of mankind.

THE REAL ISSUE OF THE WAR

The fate of a single city, the preservation of the independence of a particular nation, are the occasion, not the real cause of the present conflict. The forces of evil have been loosed in the world in a struggle between the pagan conception of a social order which ignores the individual and is based upon the doctrine of might, and a civilization based upon the Christian conception of the brotherhood of man, with its regard for the sanctity of contractual relations and the sacredness of human personality.

As President Roosevelt said on opening Congress on January 4:

"There comes a time in the affairs of men when they must prepare to defend not their homes alone, but the tenets of faiths and humanity on which their churches, their governments, and their very civilization are founded. The defence of religion, of democracy, and of good faith among nations is all the same fight. To save one, we must make up our minds to save all."

This, I believe, is the position in which all nations that cherish free institutions, individual liberty and social justice, find themselves to-day.

Canada Prepared for Effective Co-operation

I need not review the events of the last few days. They must be present in the minds of all. Despite her unceasing efforts to preserve the peace of Europe, the United Kingdom has to-day, in the determination to honour her pledges and meet her treaty obligations, become involved in war.

This morning, the King, speaking to his people at home and across the seas, appealed to all, to make their own, the cause of freedom, which Britain again has taken up. Canada has already answered that call. On Friday last, the government, speaking on behalf of the Canadian people, announced that in the event of the United Kingdom becoming engaged in war in the effort to resist aggression, they would, as soon as parliament meets, seek its authority for effective co-operation by Canada at the side of Britain.

As you are aware, I have all along felt that the danger of war was such that parliament should not be dissolved, but be available to consider any emergency that might arise.

Parliament will meet Thursday next. Between now and then, all necessary measures will be taken for the defence of Canada. Consultations with the United Kingdom will be continued. In the light of all the information at its disposal, the government will then recommend to parliament the measures which it believes to be the most effective for co-operation and defence.

That parliament will sanction all necessary measures, I have not the least doubt. Already, I have received from the Leader of the Opposition and from representatives of the other parties in the House of Commons, assurances of their full appreciation of the gravity of the situation, and of their desire to see that such measures are adopted as, in the present crisis, will best serve the national interest.

MEASURES FOR DEFENCE OF CANADA

Our first concern is with the defence of Canada. To be helpful to others, we must ourselves be strong, secure, and united. In anticipation of a state of war, the government has already availed itself of the provisions of the War Measures Act, to take essential measures for the defence of our coasts, our land and our people. As has already been announced, the militia of Canada, the naval service and the air force are already on active service.

This morning these measures were supplemented by others, including the putting into effect of the "Defence of Canada Regulations". Measures have also been taken to prevent profiteering in the necessaries of life.

In what manner and to what extent Canada may
most effectively be able to co-operate in the common
cause is, as I have already stated, something which
parliament itself will decide. All I need to add at the
moment is that Canada, as a free nation of the British
Commonwealth, is bringing her co-operation voluntarily. Our effort will be voluntary.

Appeal to Unite in National Effort

The people of Canada will, I know, face the days of
stress and strain which lie ahead with calm and resolute courage. There is no home in Canada, no family,
and no individual whose fortunes and freedom are not
bound up in the present struggle. I appeal to my fellow-Canadians to unite in a national effort to save
from destruction all that makes life itself worth living,
and to preserve for future generations those liberties
and institutions which others have bequeathed to us.

CANADA ENTERS THE WAR

The special session of parliament assembled on Thursday, September 7. The proceedings on the first day were confined to the formal opening; the following day, the debate on the address in reply to the Speech from the Throne began. In the course of the debate, the Prime Minister outlined the policy of the government regarding the war.

On September 9, the Prime Minister announced that the government would regard the adoption of the address as an authorization to recommend to His Majesty the King that His Majesty proclaim a state of war between Canada and Germany. The debate concluded the same evening. On the following morning, September 10, Canada was formally declared to be at war with Germany.

CANADA ENTERS THE WAR

I NEVER dreamed that the day would come when, after spending a lifetime in a continuous effort to promote and to preserve peace and good-will, in international as well as in industrial relations, it should fall to my lot to be the one to lead this Dominion of Canada into a great war. But that responsibility I assume with a sense of being true to the very blood that is in my veins. I assume it in the defence of freedom— the freedom of my fellow-countrymen, the freedom of those whose lives are unprotected in other countries, the freedom of mankind itself. Hitler has said: "Whoever lights the torch of war in Europe can wish for nothing but chaos." "Nothing but chaos"; that is what the leader of the Nazi party in Germany is seeking to bring upon the world to-day. And it is to prevent chaos becoming the fate of this and other lands that it becomes our duty, as citizens of Canada, to stand to a man in the defence of our country and at the side of Great Britain in the defence of freedom.

Parliament has been summoned to learn the government's policy, and I am here to-day to expound it. Following the rules of parliament, this is the first moment I have had in which to speak in the course of this debate. I shall seek to leave no doubt in the mind of anyone, if there is any doubt existing even now, as to what the government's policy is. We stand for the

7

defence of Canada; we stand for the co-operation of this country at the side of Great Britain. If this house will not support us in that policy, it will have to find some other government to assume the responsibilities of the present. We are committed to that policy. When it comes to the expression of views of honourable members from every side of this House of Commons I believe we shall find that we have the house very solidly behind us.

Fateful Consequences of Neutrality Foretold

I noticed in the press last evening that one of the German papers which is supposed to be an organ of the administration had quoted Hitler as saying that if England wished to fight she must remember that if she entered this fight the prize of victory would be the British Empire. Well, that includes Canada. There is no portion of the globe which any nation would be more likely to covet than this Dominion of Canada. There is no other portion of the earth's surface that contains such wealth as lies buried here. Nowhere are there such stretches of territory capable of feeding for generations to come, not hundreds of thousands, but millions of people.

No, Mr. Speaker, the ambition of this dictator is not Poland. At one time he said it was only the area in which there were German-speaking people. But we have seen that ambition grow. That may have been the thought in his mind some years ago, but we all know how ambition feeds upon itself; we all know how the lust for power blinds men's senses to all else. We know where and how he started. He began first with the militarization of the Rhineland. He then said—I quote Hitler's own words—he had "no thought of annexing Austria." After giving his word that there would be no further attempt at conquest, he took a part of Czechoslovakia. Then he took Moravia and Bohemia, then Memel, now Danzig and Poland. Where is he creeping to? Into those communities of the north, some of which to-day say they are going to remain neutral. I tell them if they remain neutral in this struggle, and Britain and France go down, there is not one of them that will bear for long the name that it bears at the present time; not one of them. And if this conqueror by his methods of force, violence and terror, and other ruthless iniquities is able to crush the peoples of Europe, what is going to become of the doctrine of isolation of this North American continent? If Britain goes down, if France goes down, the whole business of isolation will prove to have been a mere myth. There will in time be no freedom on this continent; there will in time be no liberty. Life will not be worth living. It is for all of us on this continent, by helping others, to do our utmost to save its privileged position.

THE FORCES OF GOOD AND EVIL

When it comes to a fight between good and evil, as the evil forces of the world are let loose upon mankind, are those of us who believe in the tenets of Christianity, and all that Christianity means and has meant to the homes and lives of men, in the present and through generations in the past—are those of us who have reflected with reverence upon the Supreme Sacrifice that was made for the well-being of mankind going to allow evil forces to triumph without, if necessary, opposing them by our very lives?

I believe the present conflict, in essence, to be just that very thing. This world, year in and year out, age after age, witnessed opposing forces contending for supremacy. They have been the forces of good and the forces of evil. To-day those forces are locked in mortal combat, and if we do not destroy what is evil, it is going to destroy all that there is of good. And what is going to become of this world as a place in which to live?

A Sense of Impending Calamity

I need not tell honourable members that the sense of impending calamity was not something which was realized all of a sudden. Three years ago the government indicated its belief in the necessity for preparedness by asking parliament substantially to increase the amounts required for the defence services of our country. I frankly confess that from that day to this the possibility of a war in which Germany or other nations would be engaged, and which might spread to all parts of the world, has absorbed most of my time and thought. Particularly have I been concerned with the position of our own country in the event of Great Britain becoming again engaged in war. I have not concealed my conviction as to what I feared might occur. Time and again when my own followers have been discussing with me many matters of major and minor importance, I have urged upon them the wisdom of keeping constantly in mind the terrible possibility of international conflict, before which all else would soon pale and be forgotten.

I have never doubted that when the fatal moment came, the free spirit of the Canadian people would assert itself, as it did a quarter of a century ago, in the preservation and defence of freedom. I have, however, been anxious that, when the inevitable hour came, our people, from coast to coast, should be as one in recognizing the magnitude of the issue and as one, in their determination to meet it. I have made it, therefore, the supreme endeavour of my leadership of my party, and of my leadership of the government, to let no hasty or premature threat or pronouncement create mistrust and divisions between the different elements that compose the population of our vast dominion, in order that our national effort might be marked by unity of purpose, of heart and of endeavour.

A STEADY PROGRESSION OF ACTS OF AGGRESSION

As honourable members will recall, when this parliament first assembled it was faced with a critical situation in Abyssinia. Ethiopia had been invaded; and the first question which confronted the present government was that of the sanctions to be imposed against Italy because of an act of aggression on her part at that time. That was in 1935. In 1936, in the spring of the year, the world was confronted with the sudden re-militarization of the Rhineland by Hitler. Before we had reached the middle of that year there was an outbreak of war in Spain, a civil war which came ominously soon after the invasion of Ethiopia. In 1937 the world witnessed the revival of the Japanese intervention in China. At the time the Spanish war threatened to embroil all Europe. With that condition on two continents, the world was faced in 1938 with the seizure of Austria by Hitler. Then came the Sudeten crisis and the campaign for the annexation of the Sudetenland, which was followed by the Munich pact in September, 1938.

It must be apparent to everyone now that, if Mr. Chamberlain had not gone to Munich when he did, on each of the three occasions that he sought to preserve the peace, war would then have broken out at that time at the instance of Hitler and his regime. What position the world would be in to-day, with the lack of preparation in different parts of Europe and elsewhere what is was, none of us, I should think, would care to contemplate.

That was in 1938. In 1939, there came in March the seizure of Bohemia and Moravia by Germany; a little later in the same month, the seizure of Memel also by Germany; then the next month, in April, the seizure of Albania by Italy; and on September 1, the invasion of Poland by Hitler and his forces.

In other words, there has been a steady progression of acts of aggression through the last five years. They point pretty clearly to some understanding and agreement between the powers involved. We have had war on all sides, a record of combined and continuous aggression. I think we may well ask ourselves from what source these acts of aggression drew their inspiration. We may well ask upon what secret understanding they may have been based, and what the world may yet witness if, in some way, this aggression is not checked.

I mention these facts for the reason that some there may be who have the impression that this war has been caused by the mere invasion of Poland and that it has to do only with a desire on the part of Germany to regain the city of Danzig. The record speaks for itself.

It discloses clearly that, in the last five years, some country or group of countries has been acting on the supposition that the great free countries of the world, "the democracies", as they are sometimes called— I confess I am getting a little tired of the use being made of the word "democracy"—were an effete lot, that they were not prepared to stand up and fight for their liberties, and that aggression was a safe method of procedure. Well, unless a pretty definite stand is taken now by those who prize their freedom, they may expect that aggression will not cease, but will continue to the limit.

Government Policy Announced and Parliament Summoned

On Friday the first of this month I gave out the following statement:

"It is now apparent that the efforts which have been made to preserve the peace of Europe are likely to prove of no avail. In spite of these efforts hostilities have begun between Germany and Poland which threaten the peace of the world. The cabinet met at nine o'clock this morning, and in accordance with the intimation given some days ago decided to have parliament summoned forthwith. A proclamation has been issued summoning parliament to meet on Thursday next, the seventh instant."

Here may I pause to point out that this statement was made before Britain was actually at war; and may I add the further statement, that such action as this government is taking to-day it is taking in the name of Canada as a nation possessing in its own right all the powers and authority of a nation in the fullest sense. The action we are taking to-day, and such further action as this parliament may authorize, are being and will be taken by this country voluntarily, not because of any colonial or inferior status vis-à-vis Great Britain, but because of an equality of status. We are a nation in the fullest sense, a member of the British Commonwealth of Nations, sharing like freedom with Britain herself, a freedom which we believe we must all combine to save.

The statement continued:

"In the event of the United Kingdom becoming engaged in war in the effort to resist aggression, the government of Canada has unanimously decided as soon as parliament meets, to seek its authority for effective co-operation by Canada at the side of Britain."

We did not decide we would have to go into war, willy-nilly. The policy as therein set forth was, we believed, that to which the Canadian people wished effect to be given. We have summoned parliament to express here, as representing the Canadian people, its will and its wish in the matter of the country entering the war voluntarily and of its own decision and right.

"Meanwhile necessary measures will continue to be taken for the defence of Canada. Consultations with the United Kingdom will be continued. In the light of all the information at its disposal, the government will recommend to parliament the measures which it believes to be most effective for co-operation and defence.

"The government has provided for the immediate issue of a proclamation under the War Measures Act in view of the existence of a state of apprehended war. The militia of Canada which a few days ago was called for voluntary service under section 63 of the Militia Act has, under section 64 of the same Act, been placed on active service. The naval services and the air force have also been placed on active service."

The statement concluded:

"The people of Canada will, I am sure, face this grave situation with calm and confidence and, above all else, in a spirit which will serve to preserve the unity of our country and the maintenance of its freedom."

BASIS OF CANADA'S WAR EFFORT

What are the measures and methods that we propose to adopt in prosecuting our effort in the defence of Canada and in co-operation with Britain? So far as co-operation is concerned our efforts will be carried out in the light of the fullest information we can obtain in regard to the whole situation, as the result of consultation with the British authorities, and of the knowledge we ourselves may possess, or obtain from other sources.

It is not possible at this stage to forecast the character and requirement of the titanic conflict which has already commenced and which threatens the peace not of Europe only but of the entire world. We know the present alignment of nations and can in some measure conceive the economic and strategic factors inherent in the present situation. We cannot, however, be certain as to what other countries may enter the conflict on one side of the struggle or the other, and the consequent readjustment both of tasks to be met and of contributions to that end. We have vivid in our memories the experience of the last war, from which we have much to learn both as to heroic endeavour to be emulated and mistakes to be avoided. It is clear, however, that in many vital respects the conditions of the present struggle differ very greatly from those of the last, and that we cannot simply assume that the methods and objectives of 1914 are applicable to 1939. We must frame our policy in the light of our knowledge of the present situation and the best information we can obtain as to the probable course of future developments. To this end, as I have already indicated, we have been and shall of course remain in close consultation with the government of the United Kingdom, so that the assistance Canada is to render, if it is to have the greatest effectiveness, shall not be unplanned and irresponsible.

Measures Respecting the Defence and Security of Canada

The primary task and responsibility of the people of Canada is the defence and security of Canada. The Minister of National Defence defined these needs in this house on February 15, 1937.

He said:

"National security, national defence, the direct defence of Canada, of our coastal areas, our ports, our shipping terminals, our territorial waters, the focal areas of our trade routes adjacent to our harbour mouths—these are the matters dealt with in these estimates."

This involves, in the first instance, military measures of defence. I have already outlined the steps which have been taken to safeguard the situation by calling out the active militia and the naval and air forces. Further measures will be taken in the directions where the need proves most imperative.

Again, we must provide for internal security and guard against sabotage, disturbance of vital military and economic establishments, and against hostile propaganda. A wide range of economic defence measures must be considered. The outbreak of war involves a tremendous upheaval both in international and in internal trade. It involves the redirection of many energies, the intensification of some forms of effort, the reduction of those less vitally necessary. It involves vigilant action to furnish the necessary financial support for the military measures to be taken, and to maintain the credit and the financial relations of Canada. Profiteering must and will be rigidly controlled. Close co-operation with the provinces and with representatives of industry and agriculture, of labour and of commerce will be established.

MEASURES OF CO-OPERATION WITH THE UNITED KINGDOM

Next, we must consider measures of co-operation with the United Kingdom. The safety of Canada depends upon the adequate safeguarding of our coastal regions and the great avenues of approach to the heart of this country. Foremost among these is the St. Lawrence river and gulf. At the entrance to the St. Lawrence stands the neighbouring British territory of Newfoundland and Labrador. The integrity of Newfoundland and Labrador is essential to the security of Canada. By contributing as far as we are able to the defence of Newfoundland and the other British and French territories in this hemisphere, we will not only be defending Canada but we will also be assisting Great Britain and France by enabling them to concentrate their own energies more in that part of the world in which their own immediate security is at stake. The British Government, in reply to the inquiry we have made, have indicated their agreement that this would be an effective and desirable means of co-operation.

We propose to co-operate in economic pressure, which is an essential factor in the situation that faces us. Measures looking to the prevention of trading with the enemy, control of essential exports and appropriate measures with regard to alien enemies, merchant ships and property will be taken. Of special and vital importance is the furnishing of supplies of all kinds to the British and allied powers, munitions, manufactures, raw materials and foodstuffs.

The urgent necessity of a constant supply of munitions, and the ability of Canada, because of its industrial equipment and its relative accessibility to the main theatres of the war, to meet these needs in great measure, are apparent. This is also a subject on which there has been consultation with the government of the United Kingdom. It may be said with assurance that a determined national effort to bring our industry and agriculture to the point of highest efficiency and to keep them at that high level will be of the utmost importance to the common cause. Specific measures of economic and financial co-operation which we propose to recommend in order to make an effective contribution in this and other fields will shortly be announced.

As regards action in other theatres of war and the

means and measures that might be taken, certain essential information touching the character of British and allied action and contemplated plans must be available before any intelligent and definitive decision could be made as to Canadian action even in the immediate future. On this all-important aspect of co-operation in defence, the Canadian Government, like the governments of other of the dominions, is in consultation with the British Government. We will continue to consult with the purpose of determining the course of action which may be regarded as most effective. There are certain measures of economic, naval and air co-operation which are obviously necessary and desirable and which it is possible to undertake without delay. I have already referred to economic measures. The information we have obtained indicates that the most immediate and effective further means of co-operation would be a rapid expansion of air training, and of air and naval facilities, and the despatch of trained air personnel. These measures we propose to institute immediately.

STRUGGLE CERTAIN TO BE LONG AND DIFFICULT

We cannot shut our eyes to the fact that the task before us may be long and terribly difficult. It is a task that will require all the strength and fortitude, all the effective organization of our resources, that we can achieve. There can be no doubt of the final outcome of the war. Whatever may be the initial trends in local actions, the resources, military and economic, on which the countries fighting for freedom can draw are fortunately greatly preponderant.

We cannot yet look forward to the conclusion or to

the peace that must some day be made; but we must from the start remember that force alone can settle nothing; that force is helpful only in so far as it insures the establishment and maintenance of enduring peace.

The efforts made after the last war to build up a new world order have tragically failed for the moment, but they have not been in vain. The people have still in their hearts the ideal of a world where change can come by peaceful means, where disputes can be settled by discussion and conciliation, and where the nations will increasingly find the interests they have in common stronger than the interests which divide them, and agree to the measure of world organization and subordination of excessive nationalism that are necessary to give expression to this conviction. We have through the operation of the League of Nations, experience of what can and cannot be done. We have a new realization of the urgency of the need, a new determination to avert the ghastly possibility of a world war every generation. The peoples of continental Europe must find in some way, through federal relationships or economic partnerships or rebirth of democratic institutions and the spirit of liberty, the art of learning to live together. The rest of the world that cares for freedom must strive in complementary ways alike for the repelling of to-day's aggression, and for the upholding of to-morrow's saner way of life.

Responsibility for the Present Conflict

I should not like to conclude without giving the house an expression of my own conviction as to where the responsibility lies for the present conflict. To help

others to understand the situation which the world is
facing, I should like to pronounce from the lips of
Hitler himself, such judgment as I may pass on Hitler
and the Nazi regime of Germany.

I have in my hand a copy of a speech delivered by
Hitler, as Fuehrer and Chancellor, in the Reichstag
on May 21, 1935. This copy was given to me by one of
Hitler's official circle when I visited Germany two
years ago. It was said to express the views of Hitler
at that time! I quote only a few of the more significant
passages.

"The blood shed on the European continent in the
course of the last three hundred years bears no proportion to the national result of the events. In the
end France has remained France, Germany Germany, Poland Poland, and Italy Italy. What dyn-
astic egoism, political passion and patriotic blindness have attained in the way of apparently far-
reaching political changes by shedding rivers of blood
has, as regards national feeling, done no more than
touched the skin of the nations. It has not substantially altered their fundamental characters. If these
states had applied merely a fraction of their sacrifices to wiser purposes the success would certainly
have been greater and more permanent. . . .

"No! National Socialist Germany wants peace because of its fundamental convictions. And it wants
peace also owing to the realization of the simple
primitive fact that no war will be likely essentially
to alter the distress of Europe. It would probably
increase it. . . .

"What then could I wish more than peace and
tranquility? But if it is said that this is merely the
desire of the leaders, I can reply that if only the
leaders and rulers desire peace, the nations themselves will never wish for war."

It is clear from this statement that it is the leaders, not the German people, who do not desire peace at this time. And that is why we have war.

"... the world war should serve as a terrible warning. I do not believe that Europe can survive such a catastrophe for a second time without the most frightful upheaval."

Hitler has deliberately brought on this war notwithstanding his conviction that Europe cannot survive such a catastrophe. To serve his ambitions he is prepared to sacrifice the whole of Europe.

"Germany has solemnly recognized and guaranteed France her frontiers as determined after the Saar plebiscite. Without taking the past into account Germany has concluded a non-aggression pact with Poland. There is more than a valuable contribution to European peace, and we shall adhere to it unconditionally. We dearly wish that it may continue without interruption and that it may tend to still more profound and friendly sincerity in the mutual relationships between our two countries. The German Reich—and in particular the present German Government—have no other wish than to live on friendly and peaceful terms with all neighbouring states. We entertain these feelings not only towards the larger states, but also towards the neighbouring smaller states. As soon as the dogs of war are loosed on the nations the end begins to justify every means. And then people soon begin to lose all clear sense of right and wrong.

"Germany has nothing to gain by a European war of any kind. What we want is freedom and independence. For this reason we were ready to conclude pacts of non-aggression with all our neighbours, Lithuania excepted.

"Germany neither intends nor wishes to interfere

in the internal affairs of Austria, to annex Austria or conclude an anschluss.

"... I consider that I owe it to my position as Fuehrer and Chancellor of the Reich not to admit a single doubt as to the possibility of maintaining peace. The peoples wish for peace. It must be possible for the governments to maintain it. ...

"We believe that if the peoples of the world can agree to destroy all their gas, inflammatory, and explosive bombs this would be a more useful undertaking than using them to destroy one another."

The address concludes with this sentence:

"I cannot better conclude my speech of to-day to you, my fellow-fighters and trustees of the nation, than by repeating our confession of faith in peace. The nature of our new constitution makes it possible for us in Germany to put a stop to the machinations of the war agitators. May the other nations too be able to give bold expressions to their real inner longing for peace. Whoever lights the torch of war in Europe can wish for nothing but chaos."

Those are the words of the leader of the German people of to-day, who has just invaded Poland after a series of acts of aggression against a number of the states with whom he said his only desire was to be at peace. Having regard to these statements, which until a year or two ago and even until the very recent past have been put forward as the profession of faith of the Nazi regime, I ask honourable members if it is possible to believe anything at all that may be said by that regime and its leader. No, Mr. Speaker. What this world is facing to-day is deception, terror, violence and force, by a ruthless and tyrannical power which seeks world domination. I say there has not been a time, the period of the last war not excepted, when the countries of the world have faced such a crisis as they face to-day.

World Slavery or World Freedom

I ask honourable members and the people of Canada: In what spirit are you going to face this crisis? Are you going to face it believing in the rights of individuals, believing in the sacredness of human personality, believing in the freedom of nations, believing in all the sanctities of human life? I believe you are. I believe that through their representatives in this parliament the Canadian people will so indicate in no uncertain way.

Some years ago, in the forties of last century, there was a bitter anti-slavery agitation in the United States. The agitation, as to whether human beings were to be slaves or were to be free, continued over the years, and finally, in the sixties, the United States found itself engaged in civil war to determine whether the nation was to be half slave and half free. That was a crisis which affected only one country on one continent. The present crisis, the crisis of 1939, affects every country on every continent of the world.

THE ISSUE

The special session of parliament concluded on September 13. The necessary appropriations for Canada's war effort were speedily voted. The government, meanwhile, proceeded with the measures required to put the country on a war footing.

On October 27, as a means of clarifying the issue in the public mind, and thereby more clearly defining the war aims, the Prime Minister delivered a nation-wide broadcast in which the Nazi mentality and methods, and the occasion and nature of the conflict were fully set forth.

THE ISSUE

SINCE the entry of our country into the war, the time of the government has been occupied with the steps necessary to place Canada on a war footing. For weeks before, as the clouds were gathering, we had quietly, but none the less effectively, been preparing for the eventuality of war. With what forethought and precision every essential detail had been anticipated became apparent the moment war broke out in Europe.

THE NATURE OF THE CONFLICT

To understand the struggle, we must first understand how the pagan conception came to dominate Germany.

For years past, we have witnessed within Germany the growth in power of a single political party which has secured not merely the control of government, but, for the time being, at least, an all but complete domination over the minds and will of the German people. This the party has been able to do by a skilfully worked out system of terrorization. Individuals who have dared to express opinions contrary to the government in power have been threatened; many have actually suffered imprisonment or death.

The party has succeeded in identifying itself with the State. It has taken the position that whatever is contrary to the policy of the party is opposed to the

27

interest of Germany. It has increased its power by propaganda specially designed to poison at their source, the springs of information and opinion. By these and other methods, the party has sought to instil in the minds of all, and particularly of the young, doctrines entirely opposed to those on which human relations are based in free countries, or on which they were based in the Germany of other times.

NAZIISM FOUNDED ON THE DOCTRINE OF FORCE

We teach our children to believe in the power of Truth and Right and Justice; in the value of a man's word, in obedience to laws framed by free representative assemblies, in the sanctity of contracts, whether between individuals or between nations. We ourselves have come to see that these concepts are the essentials of peace and freedom; that it is only in this way that human liberties can be preserved. Under the regime which has held power in Germany for nearly seven years, the youth of that country have been increasingly taught not to place their trust in the pledged word, the written contract, and the power of representative assemblies and courts to defend the right and secure freedom, but to look to Force as the one instrument in national and international relations on which to place reliance. Of the merits of any alternative to Force, there has been no opportunity for discussion or debate. Opposition has been silenced by threats, by the concentration camp, or by death. Parliament, in Germany, has ceased to exist, except when it is called to register the will of the dictator.

The political party in Germany that has thus identified itself with the State is the Nazi party. Its head is Herr Hitler. It is Naziism and Hitlerism, as thus understood, which have produced the present war, and which threaten, if not overthrown, to extend their tyrannical power to all nations.

It is necessary to keep this danger in mind in order to understand why Great Britain and France found it imperative to pledge their support to Poland. It was a pledge given in the hope that it might prevent more in the way of aggression. When Herr Hitler and the Nazi rulers who surround him disclosed their unwillingness to settle differences between the two countries by peaceful methods of conference and agreement, but, instead, made clear their determination to gain their objectives by force, Britain and France were bound to oppose, with all the resources at their command, this further employment of force.

The Rise of Naziism in Germany

How is it that the German people, many of whom love freedom and desire peace quite as much as the peoples of other countries, have come to submit to such a regime? This is a question which naturally arises in our minds. The answer to it affords the key to much that has taken place, and which it would otherwise be difficult to explain. It lies in the sort of beneficent role which, in the eyes of a large proportion of the German people, Force has actually come to assume.

Germany was slow to recover from the humiliation of defeat in the last war. The Republic which was set up in 1919 was associated in the popular mind with the shame of the peace treaty. The government of the Republic seemed powerless to cope with the social problems which followed in the wake of the war. To add to its difficulties, the discontent of the twenties began to breed Communism and to further its spread. Amid the existing demoralization, the Communist party employed its growing strength to undermine the country's social and industrial life.

It has been asserted that the Communists had little or no chance of gaining power. Many Germans, however, were afraid of the Communist influence. They had fresh in their memories, and before their very eyes, the results of the Russian revolution. Herr Hitler claimed to understand and to foresee the dangers to Germany of the Communist movement. He became a leader against it. He sought to identify Communism with Jewish control of opinion and finance. Thereby, he satisfied a bitter personal prejudice, and gained much anti-Semitic support. Powerful industrial and financial interests became his allies. Hitler and his associates came in time to be widely accepted as the champions of the German people against what he called the Jewish Communist menace.

With the aid of the financial interests, who supported him as a bulwark against Communism, Hitler became Chancellor. From that time on the political party, of which he was the head, wielded absolute power. The government of Germany became a dictatorship based upon Force. The German people were taught to view democracies with contempt.

The Threat and Use of Force Within Germany

To the youth of Germany, Hitler sought to make the doctrine of Force especially attractive. As he glorified youth, so also he glorified arms. Youth was taught that together they symbolized the future power of the

Reich. Force, the Nazis claimed, would be effective where Reason had failed. Sir Nevile Henderson, the former British Ambassador to Berlin, cites the following statement as having been made by Hitler himself:

> "If you wish to obtain your objectives by force, you must be strong; if you wish to obtain them by negotiation, you must be stronger still."

Henderson says that this remark expresses, in its most concise form, the Hitler technique.

The first use made of force by Hitler and his associates was in the internal affairs of Germany. In order to give to the Nazi party a monopoly of power in the State, not only the Communists, but Socialists, Liberals, Catholics, and even Conservative Nationalists were persecuted and their political parties suppressed. Labour unions and co-operatives were destroyed, religious bodies were terrorized, religion itself was made subservient to the pagan gospel of racial superiority. The treatment of the Jews became steadily more brutal. At the same time the increasing regimentation of the labour and resources of Germany for rearmament on a colossal scale, and with unprecedented rapidity, served gradually to end unemployment. The superficial and temporary prosperity produced by this rearmament helped to give an appearance of order to Germany and to restore its self-respect.

The Threat and Use of Force Against Other Countries

It was not long before the threat of force was tried in the international field. It was contended by Hitler

that the Treaty of Versailles had reduced Germany
to an inferior position among the nations of the world.
In addition to being stripped of a part of her territory, Germany had also been disarmed. Other nations,
it was pointed out, had retained or were increasing
their arms. Hitler told the German people that he and
his party would throw off this yoke of German in-
feriority. Rearmament was thus given a fresh excuse
and a new impetus. Germany began with all her might
to develop her military power. It is not without significance that this step was taken in defiance of treaty
obligation.

To end alleged injustices, by restoring to the German Reich peoples of German stock and territories
formerly German, was an ambition which, naturally,
made an appeal to the German people. The restoration
of the Saar territory to Germany in 1935 was Hitler's
first international triumph. Although the Saar was returned to Germany after a plebiscite, the Nazis told the
German people that, without the threat of force, the
British and French would not have agreed to the holding of the plebiscite. The incorporation of the Saar
into Germany became a symbol of the restoration of
the territory as well as of the power of the former
Reich. Such a result seemed, within Germany, to
justify an unlimited development of military strength.
From that time on, the whole of Germany was organized into a vast military machine.

THE TECHNIQUE OF NAZI AGGRESSION

Within Germany, this machine was increasingly used
to destroy individual liberty, and to place the German
people more than ever under the power of the Nazi

party which controlled and identified itself with the State. Beyond the confines of Germany, the military might of Germany was increasingly employed as an instrument of threat and terror to other nations.

The Nazi leaders were well aware that the countries of Europe generally were not anxious for another war. They assumed that this desire to avoid war would ensure the localization of conflicts, particularly those with countries immediately adjacent to Germany. On this assumption, the party began to develop its technique for the absorption, by threat of force, of those nearby countries in which there were peoples of German stock.

The technique employed was, first of all, to develop a quarrel with the government of the State to be absorbed. With passions aroused, some incident was surreptitiously fomented, demands were thereupon presented, supported by the threat of force. The demands were so framed, and so timed, as to make acceptance impossible within the limits prescribed. As a part of the technique, all opinion on the issue, except the Nazi version, was suppressed in Germany. Adverse opinion from outside Germany was excluded from the country. Worst of all, the German people were deluged by a never-ending stream of lying propaganda.

APPARENT SUCCESS OF NAZI METHODS

The technique worked with Austria. It worked again at Munich. It worked once more in the extinction of Czechoslovakia and the recovery of Memel. Hitler believed it would work in the case of Poland. On each occasion, the alleged purpose and the method were the same. The German people were told that an old wrong

was being righted, that German territories or peoples
of the Germanic race were being restored to and incorporated in the greater Reich. Each time, however,
aggression went a step farther. Germany began to include peoples who were not Germanic in origin, and
territory which had never before been German. Moreover, the conquered peoples and possessions were
utilized, as the wealth of the oppressed Jews within
Germany itself had been, to augment the growing
power of Nazidom. All the while, Hitler and his Nazi
associates continued to count on the unwillingness of
other nations, by opposing aggression, to risk setting
all Europe aflame.

Aggression pursued in this fashion worked for a
while. As, however, its real significance came to be
understood, it was realized that it constituted a threat,
not to the countries of Europe only, but to those of the
entire world. A system which deliberately and successfully defies judicial methods of righting wrongs, and
of adjusting by peaceful means national and international disputes, cannot continue without ultimately
destroying national and international order and justice.

Moreover, reliance upon Force, as opposed to Reason, inevitably brings into association with itself the
many agencies of, and evils attendant upon, terror and
violence. Gangster methods supplant the rule of law.
Sooner or later, all the powers of darkness and evil are
loosed. They gain increasing sway.

Here is the explanation of why, when Germany began to adopt toward Poland methods similar to those
which she had employed in the case of Austria and
Czechoslovakia, the British and French Governments,

first of all, earnestly worked for an adjustment of the differences by peaceful means. It explains why, later on, regardless of the cost to themselves, they found it necessary to pledge their word to Poland, and to take up arms on her behalf. It was the one and only means left of checking more in the way of German aggression.

THE NAZI AMBITION OF WORLD DOMINATION

The invasion of Poland by Germany was, as I have said, the immediate occasion, not the cause, of the present war. Germany's defiance of peaceful methods of adjusting international differences is a defiance and a threat to all peoples and countries which still seek to base their freedom upon the rule of law, the sanctity of contracts, and the sacredness of human personality. When Nazi Germany deliberately fomented the dispute with Poland, German aggression and German power had reached a place where, to save the civilization enjoyed by free countries, it became necessary for one or more of the great powers to say that Nazi aggression must cease. Great Britain and France had been driven to believe that it is better to risk all, in an effort to save those things which make life worth living, than to continue to endure the fear of unending aggression, and the gradual dominance of the world by Force.

It must never be forgotten that behind all we have seen and felt of Nazi methods and aims during recent years, lies the Nazi doctrine of racial superiority. It appears to me as the pagan parallel of the doctrine of the Divine Right of Kings. In the gospel of Hitler, the German people, the so-called Nordic race, are the chosen people. They alone have the right to rule. All other peoples are to be subordinated to the sons of Wotan. They are to dominate the world.

Although the Nazis have a single aim—world domination—the methods being employed to achieve that end are many. Against neighbouring peoples the method is aggression, conquest, and subjugation. Against more remote lands, they have proceeded by planting centres of Nazi influence. To achieve their ends, they are, as the pact with Soviet Russia has shown, even willing to aid in the spread of Communism which they formerly claimed was the enemy of civilization. They seem to believe that, by fostering world unrest, they will be assisted in the destruction of freedom, but that, in the end, the Nazis will dominate by virtue of their racial superiority.

If there was ever a doubt that the ultimate—one might almost say the immediate—aim of Nazified Germany was the domination of Europe, as a step towards world domination, that doubt has surely been removed by what was witnessed in the first six weeks of war. The highly mechanized military machine that rolled in upon Poland, and crushed the Polish armies almost as rapidly as they came into the field; the air armada which rained death and destruction from the skies on unfortified communities and civilian populations; the presence and use of submarines over the areas and on the scale on which they have been employed, were never intended for the defence of Germany against possible invaders of her territory. They are clearly the evidence of a reliance upon Force sufficiently strong to work the will of its masters in whatever direction may best serve their lust for power.

Hatred of War and Dictatorship—Efforts to Preserve Peace

May I now say a few words that are more or less personal. I have participated in the public life of Canada for many years. My views and aims are pretty well known to all of you. No one, I believe, would accuse me of being an exhibitionist, a firebrand or a jingo. If one purpose above another has dominated my life, that purpose has been the promotion and preservation of peace. In industrial and international relations, I have striven to foster good will.

I have had, all my life, a positive hatred of war. In season and out, in our own parliament, at Imperial Conferences in London, at the League of Nations in Geneva, in all our relations with other countries, I have sought to shape and to expound the policies of our country so as to remove the danger of involving Canada in war, and, if possible, to avert war itself. I have not been satisfied with adopting a merely negative attitude. I have seized every opportunity to foster, in positive ways, the friendliest relations between classes, and races, and countries, believing that only on a basis of friendship and good will could nations hope to enjoy an enduring peace.

In recent years, I have followed, with the deepest concern, political trends in some other lands. I hate dictatorship no less than I hate war. Since a love of freedom is to be found in every human breast, it has always seemed to me that, sooner or later, the yoke of dictatorship could result only in war or revolution. I have dreaded dictatorship not so much for its effect upon the peoples in the particular countries which are prepared to tolerate it, even for a time, as for its undermining effect upon the free institutions of other lands.

Dictatorship is necessarily based upon Force. Force developed in one country, unless faced by superior force elsewhere, constitutes, for other countries, an immediate and constant menace. Free nations, in order to preserve their freedom, are compelled to change their mode and method of life, to concentrate on building up armaments, or run the risk of sacrificing their very existence. That kind of thing, obviously, cannot go on indefinitely without many nations being brought to the edge of an abyss. It is upon the edge of an abyss that mankind is standing to-day. Because of Nazi Germany, the free nations have been compelled every year to devote more and more of their resources to arming. Even so, more than one free nation has already perished before our very eyes. Should Naziism triumph in Europe, what will become of freedom in other quarters of the globe?

The Need to Withstand Aggression

This is a question which I have had to ask myself over and over again, as I have watched the growing power of dictatorships in Europe, and the onward sweep of the forces of aggression. No one, I think, has been more anxious than I have to prevent Canada being drawn into the maelstrom of European conflict. No one, except the colleagues who share with me the obligations of government, carries so great a measure of responsibility for the consequences of Canada's participation in war. Had I been afraid of responsibility, I would have abandoned public life long before this. It is because I hoped that, in the end, I might use such power and influence as my position gives me, in the effort to incline the scales of international relations to the side of peace, that I welcomed the larger measure of responsibility which came with the return of my party to power four years ago. If, to-day, I am prepared to continue to lead a government, charged with the awful responsibility of prosecuting a war, it is because, contrary to every hope and wish I have ever entertained, I have been compelled to believe that only by the destruction of Naziism, and the resistance of ruthless aggression, can the nations of the British Commonwealth hope to continue to enjoy the liberties which are theirs under the British Crown, and the world itself be spared a descent into a new and terrible age of barbarism.

The growth of my own conviction has, I believe, been more or less paralleled in the minds of most of the men and women of Canada. To-day it represents the mind of Canada itself.

I doubt if two years ago the Canadian people could have been persuaded to participate in another European war. Like Britain, like France, we were determined first to exhaust every possibility of peaceful negotiation in the settlement of international differences. It was not until we beheld every structure of peace destroyed, as quickly as it was erected, that our worst fears became confirmed. We saw forces being loosed upon the world which, if not subdued and conquered overseas, sooner or later would be at our very doors.

THE PRESERVATION OF CHRISTIAN CIVILIZATION

If I were called upon to sacrifice out of my life all save one of the influences of the past, or of my present possessions, the one thing I would wish to retain is the

influence of the Christian training of my childhood
days. That has been a sheet anchor through life. Without it, life for me would lose its warmth, its beauty,
its colour, its sustaining power in times of adversity,
the inspiration of its best endeavours. It would be a
dreary, mechanical existence at best. Knowing how
true this is, I do not wish to see the young people of
our dominion deprived of so precious a heritage, nor
future generations enslaved by the false doctrines
which would rob them of it. That early Christian influence is what above all else, were it in my power so
to do, I would wish to bequeath to all who have the
battle of life to face.

The Nazi doctrine of Force is the very antithesis of
what one finds in the Christian Gospel. If it prevails,
there will be, as I see it, an end to our Christian civilization. It will prevail unless men are prepared to
sacrifice their lives in opposing it. That is why the
present war is for the Allied Forces a crusade.

The time has come when, to save our Christian civilization, we must be prepared to lay down our lives for
its preservation. The young men who are enlisting in
our forces to-day, to serve on land, on the sea and in
the air, are first and foremost defenders of the Faith.
Like others who have gone forth to battle in the past,
they are placing their lives at the service of King and
Country, but theirs is an even greater mission. It is
the preservation, for our own and future generations,
of the freedom begotten of persecutions, martyrdoms,
and centuries of struggle. It is the preservation not
alone of national and of personal freedom but of freedom also of the mind and of the soul.

THE ORGANIZATION OF CANADA'S WAR EFFORT

On October 31, in a nation-wide broadcast, the Prime Minister outlined the organization of Canada's war effort. This review, which related exclusively to measures taken by parliament and by the government affords some idea of what was involved in changing Canada's national economy from a peace-time to a war-time basis. The principles underlying the more important war measures and the measures themselves were concisely set forth. The great importance of national unity to Canada's war effort was stressed.

During the months of October and November, the Honourable T. A. Crerar, Minister of Mines and Resources, visited London, as the representative of the Government of Canada, for purposes of conference with the Government of the United Kingdom.

THE ORGANIZATION OF CANADA'S WAR EFFORT

BROADCAST, OCTOBER 31, 1939

UPON the foundations prepared by the government, and so speedily laid by parliament, we are now developing Canada's war effort. Our actions have been controlled by the belief that, if we are to avoid errors of hasty and confused action, such as led to needless sacrifice of blood and treasure in the last war, the foundations must be well and truly laid. In what promises to be a long and exhausting struggle, our contribution will be all the more effective for careful planning. Modern war is a grim business. It demands cool judgment, and a balanced strategy.

I stated in parliament last March that, in the event of Canada taking part in a war, "participation could not be passive or formal, nor would it be unplanned or irresponsible". I added that it was clear that the conditions determining the nature of participation in such a conflict had undergone a great change since the last war. I should like now to say something about those changed conditions; about the nature of the present conflict, and the policies essential to a successful prosecution of the struggle.

Those of you who have read the War Memoirs of Mr. Lloyd George, will have been impressed by the frequency of his references, throughout the four volumes, to the most fatal of all the errors of the last war. This

was the tendency to imitate, or, worse still, to follow
mechanically, what had been done in previous wars.
Mr. Lloyd George mentions again and again the failure
to realize that times change, and, with them, the
weapons and technique of war itself. His memoirs are
largely the story of his struggle against the tendency
to do things in the same old way, and to repeat the old
errors and the old mistakes.

The war of 1914-1918 is still vividly remembered by
all who lived through those years. That memory inevitably provokes comparisons. Such comparisons, for
several reasons, are apt to be misleading. Many new
weapons have been developed as a result of discoveries
and inventions made in the last war. Some of these
developments were unforeseen even at its conclusion.
When we recall that, at the beginning of the last war,
neither submarines nor aircraft played any appreci-
able part, we are better able to realize that we are
faced with a new kind of war. In 1914, governments
were still mainly concerned about the number of men
they could place in the field. What happened in 1914
should not be blindly repeated in 1939. New weapons
demand a new technique of warfare.

Many of us still recall the feeling, widespread in
1914, that the war would be over within eight or nine
weeks. We were incredulous when Kitchener prophe-
sied that it would last at least four years. To-day, we
have no such easy optimism. The most competent military authorities believe this is not likely to be a short
war. They advise that we prepare for a war of at
least three years' duration. Of course, no one can
really foretell whether it will last that long, or whether
it may go on even longer. All we know certainly is

that we must prepare for a long and terrible struggle in which staying power, the power to hold out to the end, may well be the decisive factor.

Problems of Defence and Co-operation Created by the Present War

For Canada, the present war presents problems which did not exist in 1914. We have to-day, far greater responsibilities for the defence of our own territory and, especially, our coasts. In the war of 1914-1918, the defence of Canada was a secondary matter compared with our contribution to the allies overseas. Apart from guarding the approaches to the St. Lawrence and the Atlantic coast little was required in the way of Canadian defence. The two great powers on the far side of the Pacific, Russia and Japan, were allies of Great Britain. Japan assumed the task of naval patrol in the Pacific—the task, in fact, of defending our British Columbian coast. To-day, at all times, we must be prepared, in so far as we can, to defend our western coast for ourselves. Furthermore, in the present war, submarine warfare has been faced from the outset. The problem of naval defence of the Atlantic coast and the St. Lawrence has assumed more serious proportions. Newfoundland and the French islands of St. Pierre and Miquelon stand at our very door. Their protection is not less imperative to Canada's security than to their own. We must, also, be prepared to do our share in convoying shipping. Our naval service is being called upon to play a part scarcely dreamed of in the last war, in defence of the territory and immediate interests of Canada.

In the actual defence of Canada, the air force is no

less important than the naval service. No one can tell to what extent, before the war is over, the air force, as well as the naval service, may be required to protect our coastal areas, our ports and shipping terminals, our territorial waters, and the focal areas of our trade routes adjacent to our harbour mouths. The importance of the air force for the territorial defence of Canada, though less spectacular, may become as great as its importance to the allied effort overseas.

Canadian effort at the beginning of the war of 1914-1918 was centred on an expeditionary force. Throughout the war public attention was focused on Canada's army in the field. We shall naturally follow with the keenest interest the achievements of the military forces we send overseas. However, in this war, our effort will be concerned, at least in equal measure, with the fighting forces on the sea and in the air.

The most effective contribution Canada can make in support of the allies is certain to differ greatly from our contribution in the last war. Our contribution to economic warfare may easily prove to be the most important of all. This is widely recognized in Great Britain. A leading economic journal has suggested that in addition to our traditional part as the granary of the Commonwealth, Canada may also become its arsenal. Our relative security from the hazards of air bombing, together with our relative nearness to Europe, both point in this direction.

A CAREFULLY CO-ORDINATED NATIONAL EFFORT

I come now to the outline of what, in addition to planning, has thus far been accomplished. I have indicated some of the many directions in which the present war will make demands upon our resources, both human and material. Each of these demands will be costly. The necessary money can only come from taxation and borrowing, and there are limits to both. This, next to our determination to prevent unnecessary wastage of human lives, affords the strongest of reasons why we should seek to avoid spasmodic action and unrelated activities. So far as it is possible, Canada's effort in this war must be a planned and concerted national effort.

On the outbreak of hostilities in Europe, we began consultations with the British Government in order to work out the most helpful lines of co-operation. As a result of these consultations, we were able, as soon as Canada entered the war, to proceed at once to organize our share of the joint effort.

The Military Aspect of Canada's War Effort

Our contribution to the war has two outstanding aspects, the military and the economic. I shall review first our progress on the military side.

I. The Canadian Army

When the international situation became critical, late in August, we called up the militia for voluntary service. On September 1st, a part of the militia was placed on active service in Canada. Essential measures were taken for internal security and the preservation of public order. Coastal defence armament has been manned, batteries have been added to the defences of the main seaports and terminals on both coasts, and aircraft provided for the defence of air ports and harbours. Ten thousand armed Canadians

provide garrisons for our seaports. A reserve force
consisting of two divisions and a number of additional
units has been organized with a strength of over forty-
two thousand men. The units designed for overseas
service have been selected so that all parts of Canada
will be represented. The force includes four French-
speaking infantry battalions. It is not without interest
that the Maisonneuve Regiment of Montreal, true to
the best traditions of old Canada, was amongst the
first to reach its complement.

II. THE CANADIAN NAVY

The Royal Canadian Navy, immediately at the outbreak of war, took comprehensive measures for the
defence of Canadian ports and coasts. The Royal Canadian Naval Reserve and certain naval voluntary reserves have been called up. By the middle of September, nearly six thousand officers and men of the Canadian navy and reserve, or four thousand more than
the peace-time strength, were either afloat, or at their
bases. Our destroyers made record voyages to move
to their predetermined stations. Our reserve merchant
vessels, and fishing boats, and other small craft, were
requisitioned, and are now efficiently performing their
allotted duties. Our ships on the Atlantic coast are
taking part in the convoy system, and to date not a
single ship leaving Canada has been lost. Our dock-
yards are, and our shipyards will soon be, working to
capacity. Our mine-sweepers are performing their important duties. Our regular and auxiliary fighting
ships are fully armed with torpedoes, depth charges
and ammunition. Our naval forces are, in addition,

co-operating with the British Navy in the protection of Newfoundland and the West Indies.

III. THE CANADIAN AIR FORCE

The eyes of our people have turned, with particular interest and pride, to the Royal Canadian Air Force. The air record of Canada in the last war, and the gallantry, the self-reliance, and the mechanical skill of our Canadian youth, have kindled the imagination and fired the enthusiasm of the allied nations, as well as our own. At the outbreak of war, all available squadrons were moved to their war stations, with special concentrations upon the east coast. The Air Force is at present assisting in the patrol of the shipping lanes of the Atlantic seaboard, the convoying of merchant vessels, and the varied business of national defence.

MILITARY CO-OPERATION WITH THE ALLIED FORCES

By far the most important development in the air is the agreement between the governments of Canada, Great Britain, New Zealand, and Australia, to establish in Canada advanced training facilities for pilots from all four countries. On the fifteenth of this month, a British Air Training Mission, headed by Lord Riverdale, arrived in Ottawa. They are being joined by similar Missions, now on their way from Australia and New Zealand, to work out the details of the scheme with the officials of the Canadian Government. All the countries involved, including ourselves, will be individually responsible for elementary training. Advanced training on a very large scale, involving in the first year, many millions of dollars and many thousands of men, will be concentrated in Canada. This may well mean that the final victory will be shaped on Canadian soil—for who can exaggerate the importance of this great co-operative effort in the training of men and the forging of an overwhelming air strength.

Apart from the measures for the immediate territorial defence of Canada, which had been prepared for long in advance, the problem of working out our full military effort has inevitably involved much detailed consideration. It is essential that Canada keep in step with the allied powers. To do so, we have been in constant touch with the British Government, which, in turn, has been in the closest association with the French. In order that our own and the other governments may have more complete information, one of our senior Ministers, Mr. Crerar, has recently gone to London for direct conversations with the British Government and representatives of the other governments of the Commonwealth. In our military effort, we are determined to avoid wasteful sacrifice. We are not concerned to make it spectacular; but we are vitally concerned to make it effective.

CANADA'S WAR EFFORT—ITS ECONOMIC ASPECT

I turn now from the military to the economic aspect of our war effort. In embarking upon a war, the public naturally think first of the fighting forces, and, only secondarily, of war materials and supplies. I have already shown that in modern warfare the emphasis has shifted from crude man-power to material resources and technical skill. The equipment of war: rifles, machine guns, field guns, tanks, submarines, destroyers, mine-sweepers, cruisers, battleships, and, above all, aircraft, are not only increasingly costly to produce, but they are required in ever greater quantities. War has an ever-growing appetite for munitions of all kinds: cartridges, high explosive shells, bombs and torpedoes. Troops require shelter, clothing and foodstuffs.

In order to have the tremendous quantities of supplies available at the right time, and in the right place, it is imperative that the economic life of Canada be reorganized, but not disorganized. The economic forces of the country require to be mobilized, just as the armed forces are mobilized. This task can be performed, in the main, only by the national government. Its adequate performance, however, demands the co-operation of provincial and municipal authorities, as well as of business, labour, the farmers and other primary producers, and of voluntary organizations of all kinds.

THE PRODUCTION AND PURCHASE OF MUNITIONS AND OTHER SUPPLIES

The government had not waited for the outbreak of war to tackle the problem of war purchases and supply. It was known that the organization and mobilization of the resources and industries available to Canada, in the contingency of war, would necessitate, at the outset, a survey of Canadian industry and industrial capacity. This survey was completed some time ago. At the session of parliament prior to the war, provision was made for the establishment of a Defence Purchasing Board. The Board was set up in July and had begun to function actively before the outbreak of war. War conditions demanded speedier procedure and wider powers than we felt were justified in peace time. These were given under provisions of the War Measures Act. The government, at the same time, proceeded to establish a War Supply Board, with enlarged powers and increased personnel. The organization of the War Supply Board has been completed. It will, to-morrow morning, take over the duties of the Defence Purchasing Board. The War Supply Board will continue the task of organizing and mobilizing the nation's resources and industries, and dealing with the problems involved in the handling of supplies, the construction and extension of defence projects, and the approval of contracts for equipment and supplies required by all three branches of our armed forces. Since September 8th the British Government has had a War Purchasing Mission in Canada. Arrangements have been made between that Mission and the government for the War Supply Board to act as purchasing agent in Canada for supplies for the United Kingdom. The War Supply Board will thus be responsible for the mobilization in Canada of all available resources of industrial production to meet the needs of our allies and ourselves.

The government is determined that the difficulties experienced in the last war, in securing munitions and supplies rapidly, and in adequate volume, shall not arise from any failure to provide an adequate organization, in Canada, to meet the demands of the present war. We, therefore, as I have already indicated, obtained authority from parliament to set up a separate department of Munitions and Supply, whenever it may be felt by the government that the progress of the war demands a more elaborate organization.

MEASURES TO PROTECT CONSUMERS AND TO FURTHER
PRODUCTION

Within a few hours of the outbreak of war, the government established the War-Time Prices and Trade Board to prevent hoarding, profiteering, and undue rise in prices of necessities. The duties and powers of the Board are extensive. It confers with manufacturers, wholesalers, and retailers, with a view to enlisting their co-operation in ensuring reasonable prices, adequate supplies, and equitable distribution of all necessaries of life. If deemed necessary for the prevention of excessive demand or excessive price the Board may license manufacturers or dealers or fix maximum prices. Wherever, after investigation, hoarding or profiteering has been found to exist, the Board has not hesitated, and will not hesitate, to take criminal proceedings. Special administrators have been appointed, under the War-Time Prices and Trade Board, for wool, sugar, hides and leather, and coal. It may be necessary for the Board, from time to time, to appoint other administrators to supervise trading in other commodities where such supervision is required to maintain a proper balance in the national economy and to protect the interests of consumers.

Among other agencies organized to assist the government in the mobilization of our economic resources, are an Agricultural Supplies Committee, to direct and co-ordinate the production of essential foods and fibres; and a Licensing Board, which has the function of licensing shipping. An Economic Advisory Committee has also been appointed to study economic problems as they arise during the war, and to advise the government, from time to time, in connection with the co-ordination of the work of governmental boards and agencies operating in the economic field.

THE VITAL IMPORTANCE OF FINANCE

Our whole war effort, both military and economic, at home as well as overseas, depends, as I have already said, upon finance. Without a wisely planned apportioning of our financial resources, neither our military forces nor our industrial and agricultural resources could be put to work for the defence of our cause. Internally and externally, we are, to-day, in a much better position, than was the case in 1914, to control our finances, and to ensure that the economic burdens of the war are shared equitably by all citizens. By means of our broadly-based tax system, we shall seek to meet, as the war proceeds, as much as we can of the financial costs of the war. The War Budget, although necessarily burdensome, was founded upon the very just principle of taxation—ability to pay. Upon those making profits from the war, we have placed a heavy excess profits tax.

The success of the recent short-term loan, bearing interest at 2 per cent, is a tribute to the wisdom of our financial policy. A large part of the proceeds of this war loan is being used to buy back, from Great Britain, a block of Canadian securities, bearing interest at $3\frac{1}{2}$ per cent, which the British Government wishes to sell in order to buy Canadian wheat, bacon, cheese and other primary products, as well as munitions and warlike equipment. In this way the war loan will not only be helping Great Britain, but also Canada.

Among other important financial measures, adopted

during the first month of war, has been the setting up of a complete system of exchange control, to conserve our financial resources, and particularly our supplies of foreign exchange. This measure has been generally acclaimed as the best and fairest way of preventing the dissipation of our capital into speculative or other unessential uses abroad.

OTHER ESSENTIAL AND HELPFUL FEATURES

The government has also taken measures to ensure the internal security of Canada. Provision has been made for the registration of aliens, for protection against sabotage and espionage, and for effective censorship under a Censorship Co-ordination Committee. In every aspect of Canada's war effort, my colleagues and I have taken and will continue to take all possible precautions to see that partisanship, personal influence, or political patronage provide no avenue to promotion, personal advancement, or private or corporate profit. We have, in our war effort, been greatly encouraged and materially assisted by the all but overwhelming offers of voluntary service for war work of all kinds. These unsolicited offers are a tribute to the spirit of the Canadian people. A Voluntary Service Registration Bureau has been established to co-ordinate these offers of service. Especially gratifying has been the co-operative attitude of the organizations of Canadian labour, and of the veterans of the last war.

I regret that the time at my disposal prevents me from making mention of the organization of many other phases of Canada's war effort, or of giving a fuller account of what has been accomplished. The mere outline I have given will be sufficient, I hope, to afford some idea of what is involved in changing a nation's economy from a peace-time to a war-time basis.

THE MAINTENANCE OF NATIONAL UNITY

I have said nothing whatever of our inter-Imperial and international relations. I ought, perhaps, to say that no matters have been more important nor required more careful consideration than many of the constitutional, diplomatic and political problems which the war has served to raise. It is not alone in relation to other parts of the Commonwealth and to foreign countries that questions of the kind have arisen. In its determination to sustain and further Canada's war effort, the government has found it necessary to be active on the political, as well as on the military and economic fronts. It is doubtful if Canada could have made, within the first two months of war, a more helpful contribution to the cause of the allies than that signified by the decisive pronouncement of a week ago.* Certainly nothing which has happened in our country, since Confederation, has contributed more to Canadian unity. Upon the maintenance of national unity, more than upon all else, will depend the measure of the success of Canada's effort in the present war.

---

*The reference here is to the results of the elections in the province of Quebec, 1939, on which date the electors of that province gave unmistakable evidence of their support of Canada's war effort.

THE BRITISH COMMONWEALTH
AIR TRAINING PLAN

An immediate result of the Nazi attack upon Poland was the proposal by the British Government of a joint air training plan in which the United Kingdom, Canada, Australia, and New Zealand should co-operate. The proposal was at once accepted in principle by all four countries. During October and November, Missions from the United Kingdom, Australia and New Zealand met at Ottawa with members and officials of the Canadian Government to negotiate an agreement and to work out the Plan in detail. The agreement was signed on December 17, 1939.

Later, on the same day, in a nation-wide broadcast, the Prime Minister outlined the British Commonwealth Air Training Plan.

THE
BRITISH COMMONWEALTH AIR TRAINING PLAN

BROADCAST, DECEMBER 17, 1939

I AM pleased to be able to announce that agreement has now been reached by the governments of the United Kingdom, Canada, Australia and New Zealand on a Co-operative Air Training Plan, to be known as the British Commonwealth Air Training Plan. The agreement was signed last night very shortly after midnight in my office on Parliament Hill. It is based on a proposal made to the governments of Canada, Australia and New Zealand, on September 26th, by the government of the United Kingdom.

In addition to a rapid and extensive increase in the air training programmes of each of the three dominions, the Plan visualizes joint training in Canada, in the more advanced stages, of pupils from Canada, Australia, New Zealand and the United Kingdom. The undertaking is one of great magnitude. It will establish Canada as one of the greatest air training centres in the world. Its development will result in a rapid increase in the number of air training schools in this country, and will achieve a steadily increasing output of highly trained pilots, observers and air gunners. The Plan will enable the four countries to meet the greatly increasing requirements of trained personnel for their respective air forces, and for such service as the combined forces may be called upon to perform in

59

the theatres of war. The aim, in short, is to achieve, by co-operative effort, air forces whose co-ordinated strength will be overwhelming.

ACCEPTANCE IN PRINCIPLE OF THE PROPOSAL

The Canadian Government accepted the United Kingdom proposal in principle on September 28th, that is, two days after it was received. The proposal was also accepted in principle, without delay, by the governments of Australia and New Zealand. No time was lost in making arrangements for carrying on the negotiations. Much detailed consideration obviously was necessary to ensure a co-operative scheme which would be completely co-ordinated with the development of the air forces of the different parts of the British Commonwealth engaged in the joint endeavour, and to determine its financial, administrative and other aspects.

In working out the Plan, the existing air training programmes of all four countries engaged in the discussions, were taken fully into account. As already mentioned, the Plan provides for a continuance of training in the United Kingdom, for an enlargement of the training programmes of Canada, Australia and New Zealand, and for a joint training programme in Canada. As the United Kingdom proposal contemplated joint training to be carried on in Canada, it was appropriate and, in fact, essential that the details of the programme should be worked out at Ottawa.

THE NEGOTIATION OF THE AGREEMENT

The agreement in all its details was worked out in the most friendly spirit, and, considering the intricacy of the problems to be solved, with remarkable speed. In the case of the Missions from Australia and New Zealand, and particularly in the case of the Mission from the United Kingdom, continuous conference by cable was necessary in matters requiring the consideration and authorization of their respective govern ments. The Canadian negotiators were in the fortu· nate position of being in immediate contact with their colleagues in the Cabinet, and the government itself was in a position to reach decisions with a minimum of delay. On some of the more important matters of policy direct negotiations between the governments concerned, were also necessary.

By November 27th, some three weeks after the arrival in Canada of the New Zealand Mission, we were able to announce that a basis of agreement had been reached for submission to the governments concerned. The time that has elapsed since has been devoted to an elaboration and precise definition of the details of the plan, and to the drafting of the agreement in its final form.

THE OBJECTIVE OF THE PLAN

The broad problem was to decide on the speediest and most effective means of training the maximum number of pilots and airmen to meet the exigencies of war. In working out the agreement, Canada, Australia and New Zealand had, necessarily, to keep in mind local defence considerations, such as the training, equipment and service of the pilots and other air personnel required to keep up their own air defences.

It was, of course, not contemplated that the requirements of Australia and New Zealand for home defence

would be met out of the personnel trained in Canada.
It was realized, however, that, as was the case with
Canada, the training facilities in these two countries
would be capable of training more personnel than
would be required for local purposes. To reach the
main objective, namely, the rapid training of the
greatest number of pilots and airmen, the facilities in
these countries, in excess of local needs, are to be used
to train Australians and New Zealanders for service
overseas with the Royal Air Force. The existing training facilities in the United Kingdom will continue to
be used by the Royal Air Force.

THE JOINT TRAINING PROGRAMME

Under the agreement as it relates to joint training
in Canada, the programme of training of personnel for
the Royal Canadian Air Force, already enlarged since
the outbreak of war, will be vastly increased. The
Canadian training programme will be merged with the
programme of joint training in Canada. In this way,
co-ordinated air training will proceed simultaneously
in all four countries.

The Joint Air Training Programme provides for the
training of many thousands of pilots in Canada each
year, about three-fifths as many air observers, and a
slightly larger number of air gunners than pilots. The
pilots, of course, are those who actually operate the
planes. The observers handle the reconnaissance
cameras and the bomb sights and as well do the navi-
gating. The gunners use the machine guns in action,
and also act as wireless operators.

The facilities in Canada will be used, in varying de-
grees, by all four parties to the agreement. Practically

all air recruits in the United Kingdom will be trained at home. In Australia and New Zealand, all air recruits will receive their initial and elementary flying training at home. Most of the Australian pupils and some of the New Zealand pupils will also receive advanced training in their own countries. Under the agreement, however, about one-fifth of the pupils to receive advanced training in Canada will come from the other two dominions. Some pupils will be received from the United Kingdom, Newfoundland and elsewhere. The great majority of the pupils will, however, be Canadians.

THE EXTENT OF THE TRAINING ESTABLISHMENT

Schools will also be needed, at the outset, for training instructors and administrative staffs. And before the training programme is brought to full capacity, ground crews and maintenance staffs will be required in large numbers to man the various schools and establishments. Repair and equipment depots, headquarters and commands, recruiting centres and records offices will also be required. In addition to the 58 schools for the training of pilots, observers and air gunners, and schools needed, at the outset, for training instructors and administrative staffs, several much larger schools will also be required to train the personnel for ground crews and maintenance staffs. The total number of schools required, in Canada, for the Joint Training Programme will be 67.

Nearly 40,000 officers and men will be required to man all the various schools, depots and other parts of the organization when it is in full operation. This will include about 2,700 officers and about 6,000 civilians. The remaining 30,000 will be members of the air force other than officers. These numbers do not include the pupils undergoing training, who will also be numbered in thousands. Many of the airmen required for training the pupils will be mechanics and other skilled artisans, who constitute ground crews and maintenance staffs.

For the programme of joint training full use will immediately be made of the existing facilities of the Royal Canadian Air Force, as well as of facilities generously made available by Trans-Canada Air Lines. However, to put the extensive programme into full operation, a great deal of construction and production will be necessary. Throughout the country, about a score of existing air fields will have to be enlarged, and some sixty odd new air fields constructed. The schools will be established in different parts of Canada. Large supplies of equipment, and stores of various kinds, will be required to furnish the schools, and also the equipment and repair depots. The construction and other industries of Canada may be relied upon to meet effectively the demands which this programme will involve.

ADMINISTRATION OF THE JOINT TRAINING PROGRAMME

Under the terms of the agreement, the Joint Air Training Programme which is to be carried out in Canada, is to be administered by the government of Canada. The organization and executive command of the training schools is entrusted to the Royal Canadian Air Force. For the general supervision of the Joint Air Training Programme, a Supervisory Board will be established in Canada. The Board will supervise the financial administration of the programme. It will also, from time to time, inspect the progress being made in the setting up of the organization, and the carrying out of the training.

All four governments will co-operate in the provision of staff and teaching personnel. The staff officers and instructors from the United Kingdom, Australia and New Zealand will, during their period of service in Canada, hold temporary appointments in the Royal Canadian Air Force. This further co-operative arrangement should go far to assure the successful working of the Joint Air Training Programme.

The Progress Already Made

The government has not awaited the conclusion of the present agreement to begin work on the development of the additional air training facilities which the Plan contemplates. Considerable progress has already been made. The Royal Canadian Air Force schools at Trenton and Camp Borden have been converted into schools for the training of instructors. For some weeks past they have been in use for that purpose. The air training facilities, which were being developed on a less extensive scale before the war, are being brought rapidly to completion. Of about 125 air fields already developed in Canada, 42 are up to the standard set by Trans-Canada Airways. Many of these will be used for the Joint Training Programme. Under arrangements made with the provincial governments, the highways staffs of all the provinces have been used for surveying additional aerodrome sites. Full advantage has been taken of the favourable weather, and most of the sites have already been surveyed. The War Supply Board has anticipated the requirements of the programme and has organized production to meet them.

The enormous variety of equipment required for the programme is being listed in detail, so that orders may be promptly placed. To prevent delays in obtaining supplies required from outside Canada, protective orders have already been placed. Now that the agreement is in force the War Supply Board will immediately begin to let the necessary contracts. Plans for the schools have already been prepared, and no time will be lost in their construction. It will thus be seen that the time spent in working out all essential features of the agreement has, in reality, not interfered with the development of the programme itself. Canada is more than ready for the large task ahead.

Arrangements for Active Service

The new programme is of such magnitude, that some little time must necessarily elapse, while schools are being built, equipment obtained, and the training of additional instructors completed, before student pilots, observers and air gunners can be accepted for their training, and before the first pilots and observers, trained under the scheme, will be sufficiently skilled to proceed to the theatres of war.

In the meantime the United Kingdom Government, appreciating the desire of the Canadian people to be represented as soon as possible by an Air Force Unit on active service in Europe, has arranged for the immediate formation of a squadron to be commanded by a squadron leader of the Royal Canadian Air Force. All the pilots in the squadron will be Canadian. The Canadian commander and pilots will be selected from

Canadians at present serving with the Royal Air Force.

The formation of this squadron has been made possible by the practical co-operation, in the training of air personnel, in recent years between the Royal Canadian Air Force and the Royal Air Force. This co-operation has resulted in the presence in the Royal Air Force of a considerable number of Canadians, some of whom, as you are aware, have already achieved distinction in the present war.

Perhaps I should mention here that, under the Commonwealth Air Training Plan, provision has been made, after their training is completed, for the identification, in the field, of the pupils with their respective dominions, either by the method of organizing dominion units and formations, or in some other way.

THE RELATION OF THE AIR TRAINING PLAN TO CANADA'S MILITARY EFFORT AS A WHOLE

In embarking upon the vast co-operative enterprise, envisaged by the Commonwealth Air Training Plan, the government had naturally to give the most careful consideration to the Plan in its relation to Canada's military effort as a whole. This aspect was, of course, very fully discussed with the government of the United Kingdom. It is obviously all-important that our effort should be co-ordinated with the effort of our allies in a single strategic plan for carrying on the war. When the Plan, in its broad outlines, was proposed by the government of the United Kingdom, it was stated that the immense influence which the development and realization of such a great project might have upon the whole course of the war, might even prove decisive.

On October 10th, at the time of announcing agreement by the several governments on the principle of the proposal, I stated that "the government of the United Kingdom has indicated its opinion that with the facilities which Canada possesses this co-operative effort may prove to be of the most essential and decisive character."

The United Kingdom Government has since informed us that, considering present and future requirements, it feels that participation in the Air Training Scheme would provide for more effective assistance towards ultimate victory than any other form of military co-operation which Canada can give. At the same time the United Kingdom Government wishes it to be clearly understood that it would welcome no less heartily the presence of Canadian land forces in the theatre of war at the earliest possible moment.

You will recall that, on September 19th, the government announced that a division was being organized for service overseas, and, as you are aware, no time is being lost in our endeavour to meet the wish of the United Kingdom for the early despatch of an Expeditionary Force.

THE REAL CONTRIBUTION

I have spoken of the magnitude of the Joint Air Training Plan, of what it is likely to mean in numbers of men to be trained, and in additional financial outlay upon Canada's war effort. It is well, however, to remember that, in the vast expansion of air power which Canada has undertaken, in collaboration with her partners in the British Commonwealth, something wholly different, and much more vital than numbers or material wealth, is involved. It is the lives of our young men which are being pledged. Like our soldiers and our sailors, the pilots and airmen who are to be trained in thousands, are going forth to battle to risk their lives in conflict with forces more sinister than any the world has hitherto known.

To-night, I am speaking particularly of those belonging to the Royal Canadian Air Force. The young men, equally with others of maturer years with whom they will be associated, are, I am convinced, fully aware of the appalling nature of the situation facing the world to-day, and of what it will demand by way of sacrifice ere peace is again restored. It is not in a spirit of adventure that they are pressing forward in such numbers. Rather are they enlisting in the spirit of the crusaders of old, prepared, if need be, to give their lives for what, to them and to us, is holy and sacred—the birthright of liberty and happiness in a free land. This fortitude and devotion must be guarded and protected by every power we possess.

In making provision for this vast undertaking, the government has done so, in the knowledge that nothing can be left to haste or to chance. The intricate machine must be perfect. In every phase of their work, the men must be trained by the highest skill, and under the best conditions it is possible for the country to provide. In no other arm of the defence services is a man obliged to rely more completely upon his own initiative, his own knowledge, and his own judgment. It is the possession of these qualities in such large measure which has given to Canadians the reputation as airmen they already enjoy. Those who enlist in Canada's air force may be depended upon to do their part, however perilous it may be. We must do ours to assist them in every possible way, by adequate training and proper equipment, and by all the influences for good by which it is possible to surround their lives.

The Mission of the Airman

I need not say to those who may come from other lands to receive their training, how warmly they will be welcomed during their brief stay in our midst. I know something of the heart of the Canadian people. I am sure, therefore, that our homes will be as open to them as they are to those of our own land, with whom they are already united as brothers, in an heroic effort to serve the world's need at this hour of its greatest peril.

Let there be no mistake about the significance of the present war. It is a veritable struggle for existence. On its outcome will depend the fate not of Britain alone, nor even, it seems to me, of the British Empire, the fall of which would shatter the world, but of Humanity itself, in all its higher aspects. To save mankind from such a catastrophe, the airmen of the British Commonwealth, whether setting their course by the North Star or the Southern Cross, are dedicating their lives. To hasten the day when peace may be restored is, I believe, the governing motive of all our forces, whether on sea, or land, or in the air.

NATIONAL UNITY AND THE DEFENCE
OF FREEDOM

The day the Air Training Agreement was signed the first contingent of Canadian troops landed in Britain. A second contingent landed at the end of the year.

On January 25, 1940, parliament reassembled. It was dissolved the same day and a general election campaign ensued. On March 26, the government was returned with an increased majority.

In the course of the campaign the Prime Minister, in a series of radio addresses, set forth important aspects of Canada's war effort, and factors contributing thereto. The following excerpts from these addresses throw light upon the government's policies for the preservation of national unity and the defence of freedom.

NATIONAL UNITY AND THE DEFENCE
OF FREEDOM

BROADCASTS, FEBRUARY 7, MARCH 21 AND 23, 1940

WHEN parliament concluded its Special War Session in September last, the Canadian people knew that Canada was united. What was of equal importance, there was left on the minds of the peoples of Europe the clear impression of a country at one in its determination to put forth a supreme national effort towards the winning of the war.

The reality of Canadian unity, in carrying on the war, was splendidly confirmed and re-inforced just six weeks later. On October 25th, the people of the province of Quebec, with a voice which carried across the Atlantic, gave their answer to a challenge which had thrown suspicion on their loyalty. Her people could not have proclaimed more conclusively, at any time, or in any way, their unity with the rest of Canada in support of the war effort of the federal ministry.

I shall always regard this twofold demonstration of Canadian unity, this evidence of the common determination of all Canadians to share in the struggle and the sacrifice, as the greatest of the contributions that, in the early stages of the conflict, Canada could possibly have made towards the winning of the war. As we preserve our national unity, so shall we increase our national strength.

How Canadian Unity Might Have Been Destroyed

It will add to our understanding of what is essential to the prosecution of Canada's war effort if we recognize, at once, that this demonstration of unity, in parliament, on the part of the people's representatives, and, in the province of Quebec, by the people themselves, was not born of the moment, and did not arise wholly of itself. It was the result, in no uncertain measure, of the known policies of the present administration, policies which, over many years, in matters of war or peace, have been clearly shown to be in accord with the will of the Canadian people.

That unity did not come from committing Canada to war before parliament had made its decision. It was not brought about by agreeing to send expeditionary forces overseas, before parliament had decided that Canada should participate in war, and had appropriated moneys for its prosecution. It was not brought about by the government seeking from parliament, in time of peace, the appropriation of huge sums of money for military expenditures in preparation for Canada's participation in a European war. Our unity was not maintained by committing Canada to fight in Europe, before, or at the time of the Munich conferences, or even after Czechoslovakia was invaded, when, as we now know, the British Government itself was unwilling to take that step. It was not achieved by declaring that, without consulting either the parliament or the people of Canada, the government would commit this country to fight at any time, at any place, in any cause, if Britain went to war. Least of all was it brought about by pledges to extend the life of parliament in a time of war without any reference to the people, or to form a so-called "national" government that might enforce conscription or disfranchise many classes of Canadian citizens. The memories of those experiences in the last war are still bitter in the minds of the Canadian people.

How Canadian Unity Was Achieved

Unity was made possible by none of these things. On the other hand, it was made possible, and it was achieved by the assurances given the people of Canada, year in and year out, that if my colleagues and I could prevent it, none of these things would happen. We were determined that parliament, or the people themselves, would decide whether Canada should participate in war. That assurance I gave the Canadian people repeatedly. I kept that promise. And I held this country to that course, steadfastly, patiently, and honourably, in spite of criticism, in spite of abuse, and in spite of aggressive demands that I should break so solemn a trust.

I knew as you must know, that, without disastrous results, we could not have entered the war, except as a united nation. I know, and you know that we cannot continue at war, at least with the strength we all desire, except as a united nation. I believe that every fair-minded citizen will agree that the policies which have united Canada are the policies which will keep our country united.

Canada's War Effort the First Consideration

No government, charged with the duty of carrying

on Canada's war effort, and, at the same time, the regular business of parliament could, in addition, be expected to face two political campaigns—one carried on in parliament itself before dissolution, another in the country after dissolution—and thereby almost certainly postpone the decision of the electors until the allied cause had reached a new and terrible emergency.

The responsibility for recommending the dissolution was mine. I took that responsibility in pursuance of my conception of my duty. I did so because I believed it to be right, and in the interest of this country. Above all else, I acted as I did in order that the unity of parliament might be preserved in the eyes of the world.

I knew that a general election had to come—so did our political opponents. I believed that it ought, if possible, to be over before the spring offensive. I believed that it ought to be brought on before roads were broken up and became impassable. I believed that it ought to come before our men in England went to France. I believed it ought to come before our second Division left this country. If parliament had been permitted to carry on to the end of March or April, and had, thereby, rendered inevitable a general election at a time when our men were facing all the horrors of concentrated warfare, I would have been told, and rightly so, that I was not fit to be the leader of the government, for allowing matters to drift in that way.

EFFORTS TO MAINTAIN PEACE IN EUROPE

I have long held the belief that conditions in Europe could not continue to go, as during the last four years they had been going, from bad to worse, without the moment coming when Europe itself would burst into flames and freedom everywhere be menaced. Holding that belief, I have done all that was within my power, and have sought to have done all that was within the power of this country, to avert such a catastrophe by fostering, everywhere and always, policies of international understanding, friendship, and good will. At the same time, I have had continually to face the prospect of the failure to maintain peace. I have also had to consider the possible coming of the day when Britain and France might be drawn into a great conflict for the preservation of their freedom and, indeed, of their very existence. I have had, all the while, to ask myself how best our country could be kept united, and its policies so shaped that, if the moment ever came for Canada to declare what part she was prepared to take in a world struggle to thwart aggression and to preserve freedom, she could speak with the single voice of a united people.

Efforts to Preserve Unity in Canada

I think I know something of the love of liberty which resides in the breast of every Canadian. I think I know something, too, of what men and women, of every part of Canada, of every class, and race, and creed, feel they owe to the manner in which their liberties have been secured under British institutions in our free association as a free nation in the British Commonwealth. I have, therefore, never doubted the singleness of mind and purpose with which we would all be prepared to play our part in any struggle which threatened our freedom. My task was to see that no false step, no extreme policies or measures, no hasty action should be allowed to destroy, in advance, either the clearness of vision of our people, or its power for action. I was determined that, if the moment for decision ever came, no cleavages of opinion, in parliament or in the country, should frustrate Canada's power to put forth her utmost effort.

The only absolute proof of any course of action is to be found in its results. You will recall my repeated assurances that Canada would participate in war only after a decision by parliament or the people; also, my refusal last year to allow a general election to be brought on in July or August, though strongly pressed by the Leader of the Opposition, and many of my own following, to dissolve parliament at that time. You will also recall how speedily parliament was summoned into special session at the moment of the crisis. You know the unanimity which marked the proceedings of parliament and its momentous decision. You know what effect all those things have had upon the continued unity of this nation in a time of war. Knowing all these things as you do, I ask you, my fellow-countrymen, has the course which I have pursued over the years I have been in office, as the leader of the government of this country, not been the right, and, indeed, the only wise and proper one? Quite apart from myself, if you will permit me to say so, you will do well, I believe, to judge of the future in the light of the past.

The People to Decide

The people of Canada are being asked to decide through what government, and as a result of what policies the will of the people of Canada is likely to be carried out most completely and effectively in the prosecution of the war effort. That war effort, as I have said, has been developed upon foundations carefully prepared. It has been furthered by steady, persistent and patient labour. We have had the experience of the last war to guide us. With that experience illuminating the course which we have had to follow, we have used every effort to avoid the errors of haste and confusion, and the needless sacrifice of blood and treasure that is their inevitable result. In a struggle that is certain to be long and exhausting, our contribution will be effective to the extent that it is carefully planned in close co-operation with that of our allies.

The decision is yours. It is not your representatives in parliament who are now being asked to decide on the present and future of this country at a time of war. It is you, yourselves, who are not only the masters of parliament, but, as never before, the masters of your own fate.

Measures Taken to Meet Situation

Let me recall to you, very briefly, some of the achievements of the present government. In peacetime, we had the courage to multiply the defence estimates—and when I say courage, I mean that very thing. Because even our opponents will admit that it takes courage to tax a peaceful and peace-loving democracy for defence against a war remote from our shores. We rebuilt our national defences; we reorganized the air force; we built the Trans-Canada Air Lines; we established the Bank of Canada as a truly national institution; we found for our producers

wider markets, we greatly increased Canada's trade
and we established the friendliest of relations with our
immediate neighbour. We did much, as well, to bring
Canada and Britain closer than ever together.

Since the outbreak of war, we have organized agriculture to meet war conditions. We have saved workers
and merchants from the disaster of falling international exchange, and the inflation of Canadian money.
We have protected the worker and the housewife from
an undue rise in the price of the necessities of life.
We have equipped and sent overseas soldiers and airmen. Our second division is training in Canada. We
greatly strengthened the army and the Royal Canadian Navy. We have played the major part in the
establishment of the Commonwealth Air Training
Plan. I dislike prophecies, but I suggest that, as you
watch events develop, you remember my words, and
the words of British statesmen, that final victory may
well be shaped by that great and powerful instrument.
We have published in the open light of day every contract made for the purchase of war supplies.

To assist in victory, we have brought to the service
of Canada outstanding men of other parties, and of no
party. We have made merit the sole criterion of promotion in the armed forces. We have allowed no man
and no group of men, however powerful, to use the
national calamity for scandalous profit making.

We began at the side of Britain and France in full
understanding. We remain there to-day. We have succeeded in maintaining a united Canada. The traditional loyalty of our French-speaking compatriots has
once again inspired us with a sense of national unity.

They too, stand side by side with English-speaking Canada, with Britain and with France, in defence of altar, home and the elemental rights of mankind.

THE VOICE OF CANADA

While the war lasts, you and I, no matter what our burdens may be, will be inspired by the knowledge that young Canadian men, like their fathers before them, are once again willing to offer life itself upon the altars of nationhood and humanity. We will do our utmost to make our endeavours worthy of them. When the war is over, the cause of peace will also need the help of Canada. It will need the united authentic voice of this nation speaking to all nations through a strong government. For the voice of Canada is the voice of the new world. It is, moreover, the voice of a young and free nation which is giving of its best in the cause of human freedom. It is the voice of generosity, good will, reconciliation, healing and Christian brotherhood.

AN ELECTION IN TIME OF WAR

Criticism of the dissolution has, from the beginning, been voiced by those who were disappointed and frustrated by the unsuccessful attempt to prolong the life of parliament with the object of forming a union government. You will recall how many were asking: "Why have an election at all in time of war?" Perhaps you have been among the number who have felt that an effort should have been made to continue parliament in existence indefinitely. Parliament could only have been kept in existence beyond five years by over-riding the Constitution, and by depriving you of the right to choose whom you wished to manage your affairs in time of war. Had members of the House of Commons joined in extending the life of parliament, without authority from the Constitution or from you, they would have completely usurped all your rights and powers.

Abraham Lincoln, at the time of the great civil war, was faced with the problem of an election in war-time in circumstances even more difficult. The Constitution of the United States calls for a presidential election every four years. The Civil War began in April, 1861. The presidential elections were due in November, 1864. Lincoln had to decide whether he and his colleagues would override the Constitution and extend their own term on the pretext that the Constitution was not framed to cope with civil war. Lincoln maintained that failure to hold the elections would be an admission that the rebellion had succeeded, and that America's free institutions had already been destroyed in a war for freedom. "We cannot," he said, "have free government without elections." The elections were held. Lincoln and his government were returned, and the world was shown that, even in the midst of a civil war, democracy and freedom could be maintained.

I venture to say that when Tuesday next is past, it will be the proud boast of the people of this country, if not indeed of the whole British Empire, that Canada has added another chapter to the history of democracy in the new world. For our country will have shown, that under British parliament institutions, it is also possible for a free people, at a time of war, to preserve their electoral freedom and the fundamental liberties which is secures.

THE LATE LORD TWEEDSMUIR

On February 11, 1940, His Excellency the Right Honourable Baron Tweedsmuir, the Governor-General, died during the course of the general election campaign. On the evening of that day, the Prime Minister broadcast a tribute to Lord Tweedsmuir's memory. This he supplemented by a further appreciation which appeared in the press of Canada on the following morning.

Upon Lord Tweedsmuir's death, the Chief Justice of Canada, the Right Honourable Sir Lyman Duff, was appointed Administrator. Sir Lyman filled the office of Administrator until the arrival at Ottawa, on June 21, of the Right Honourable the Earl of Athlone.

THE LATE LORD TWEEDSMUIR

BROADCAST, FEBRUARY 11, AND CONTRIBUTED TO THE PRESS
FEBRUARY 12, 1940

To-NIGHT, in the City of Montreal, there died a great and a good man, John Buchan, 1st Baron Tweedsmuir. With heart-felt sorrow, and in fulfilment of a sad duty, I am called upon to inform the people of our country that the life of His Excellency came to its earthly close shortly after seven o'clock.

In the passing of Lord Tweedsmuir, the people of Canada have lost one of the greatest and most revered of their Governors-General, and a friend who, from the day of his arrival in this country, dedicated his life to their service.

To his great task Lord Tweedsmuir brought wisdom, experience, the grace of words and a generosity of heart which found expression in a wide human sympathy and understanding. He came to know and to share the feelings and the aspirations of the Canadian people in all parts of the Dominion. He visited them on many occasions in the East, in the West, and in the Far North, and was never happier than when he shared the simplicities of their joys and their labours.

Out of that knowledge and understanding, there came an enthusiasm for this country, its institutions, its traditions and its people almost unique in our history. And if Lord Tweedsmuir knew the Canadian people as few, if any, Governors-General had known them before, the Canadian people learned to know him and to hold him in unsurpassed affection.

There is not a home in our Dominion which will not be saddened by the loss which our country has sustained; not a part of the British Commonwealth of Nations which will not recognize our bereavement as its own. The world itself has suffered in the passing of one whose great sympathies and talents were dedicated to the service of mankind.

He was, like so many great men of his race, a son of the manse. Christian ideals moulded his life and guided his footsteps; and it is an inspiration to recall that, on his last public appearance as Governor-General of this country, one week ago to-day, he read the Lesson in St. Andrew's Presbyterian Church in this city of Ottawa, humbly proclaiming to all men his unshaken belief in the faith of his fathers.

In the discharge of every public duty, Lord Tweedsmuir was fidelity itself. Cut off as he has been in the height of his powers, one can only believe that in the providence of God, he had completed the work which here it had been given him to do.

To the King, in the passing of His Majesty's representative in our Dominion, our country extends an expression of its profound sorrow. No Sovereign ever confided a great trust to a more faithful servant.

To Her Excellency, the Lady Tweedsmuir, to her daughter, to her three sons who to-day serve their King as their father did before them, Canada offers its deepest sympathy on this day of national mourning.

Canada was proud to have in her midst a great scholar who touched life at so many places and touched nothing which he did not adorn.

Lord Tweedsmuir's books brought refreshment, enlightenment and solace to hundreds of thousands of our citizens. His speeches, which always enshrined the best thoughts uttered in the best way, were models of matter and form. Whether he was speaking to learned societies, to professional organizations, to old Canadians in the East, or to-day's Canadians in the West, he gave them an inspired vision of the strength of democracy and of the true meaning of nationhood. Many a fisherman and farmer, prospector and trapper will mourn, in his passing, the loss of a great-hearted gentleman, who once brought humour, humanity and sympathy to the lonely places of this broad land.

As a poet, a biographer and a teller of tales, he never forgot that the true end of literature is "the notation of the human heart".

At the beginning of the century, Lord Tweedsmuir had been one of that brotherhood of far-sighted men who worked for racial conciliation and national freedom in South Africa. His experience, joined with his knowledge of history and his intuitive appreciation of the nature of free British institutions, had equipped him ideally as the direct constitutional Canadian representative of His Majesty the King. From the correct conception of that high office, he never departed in thought, word, act or deed.

Lord Tweedsmuir's own career was an inspiration to Canadian youth. His courage, his perseverance, his steadiness of purpose and his amazing industry seemed to typify the virtues of the Scottish race at their noblest and best.

Within a frame that was never robust was set an indomitable heart. He found time and energy to become a soldier, a statesman, a historian, a poet, a novelist, an orator and a man of affairs.

Many will recall Lord Tweedsmuir's recent rectorial address to the University of Edinburgh. Taking his title from *The Pilgrim's Progress,* he called it "The Interpreter's House". In it, at its conclusion, he asked, for the members of his university, the answer to the prayer of Socrates: "Grant me to become beautiful inwardly, and that all my outward goods may prosper my inner soul." I have often thought how abundantly that prayer was answered in the life of His Excellency himself. Wherever he had his habitation in Canada, whether in Rideau Hall or in the Citadel of Quebec, or under any roof great or humble, that habitation became also "The Interpreter's House". For all his great arts and talents, wherever he was, were devoted to an understanding of the people, and to the interpretation of all that was best in French and English, East and West, new Canada and old Canada.

On more than one occasion Lord Tweedsmuir expressed the wish that he might be truly called a Canadian. Hundreds of thousands of our citizens who came under the influence of his wise gentleness and his humble courtesy were more than willing to claim him as their own. I am sure he would be proud that his epitaph graven on the hearts of our people should mark the grief of Canada at the loss of her adopted son who knew her ways and loved them.

THE SPRING OF 1940—CANADA'S WAR EFFORT

Immediately after the elections, the Minister of National Defence, Hon. Norman McL. Rogers, visited Britain and France to discuss further measures of co-operation with the governments of both countries and to inspect the Canadian forces in Britain.

In the interval between the elections and the opening of the new parliament, the Prime Minister visited the President of the United States at Warm Springs, Georgia.

Parliament met on May 16, 1940. Its proceedings were dominated by the anxieties occasioned by the great German offensive on the nations of Western Europe which had already begun. On May 20, the Prime Minister gave the House of Commons a review of the situation as it had developed prior to the reassembling of parliament together with a comprehensive outline of Canada's war effort as existing at the time.

THE SPRING OF 1940—CANADA'S WAR EFFORT

THE HOUSE OF COMMONS, MAY 20, 1940

THE character of the enemies of the human race against whom we and our allies are arrayed has been unmasked in all its barbarity and violence.

Within a period of eight months the tyrants of Germany have become the masters of Poland, Denmark, a great part of Norway, Holland, and the chief cities of Belgium. By weight of men and equipment they have brought devastation to the weak and the unoffending. Within the last few days their armed forces have made a deep incursion on the soil of France, and the German Reich is now preparing new attacks upon Britain from the lands which Nazi brutality has violated. Words of passion and indignation will effect nothing. Knowing what the enemy has been and is doing, we must consider what we are doing and what we can do to meet him.

My purpose, therefore, to-night is to review as concisely as possible what Canada has done and is doing, and to indicate what further action the government has taken or proposes to take to meet the danger which threatens our allies and ourselves.

Some of the measures which have been taken and will be taken cannot, for reasons which will be obvious, be divulged at all at this time. Some must necessarily remain but partially indicated. Within the limits imposed by military necessity there will be no secrecy.

The greatest crisis in the history of the British Commonwealth is not the occasion for partisan congratulations or for partisan criticism. We are concerned not with the past but with the present and the uncertain clouded future. The task which is ours is a task for all Canada, not for any section or group of Canadians. It needs and will need the utmost vigour and wholehearted assistance on the part of each and every one of us.

From a Peace-time to a War-time Economy

It has not been a simple matter for this country to move from an economy of peace to an economy of war, just as it has not been easy for the democracies of Europe who once hoped for peace, to make preparations against an autocracy that has consistently hoped for war and planned it.

The record of the war effort of this country and an outline of the plans which we have initiated and proposed to initiate will be unfolded. Vainglorious justification is as foreign to the spirit of this solemn hour, as is carping and hysterical criticism. All I ask is that, as this house surveys the government's record and the government's plans, the record and the plans be placed in their proper perspective and examined and assessed as a whole.

The world has greatly changed since 1914. Canada has changed with it. Our national status has changed. Our political responsibility has changed. Our financial position has changed. Our industrial capacity has changed. The problems of local defence and overseas activity have been revolutionized by the new range, effectiveness and destructive power of aircraft, submarines, mechanized weapons and military equipment. The machine of war more than ever dominates the man at war. Military power can no longer be resolved in terms of the number of men enlisted.

The final result of all these factors of change, the rise of air power and the elimination of distance, cannot yet, of course, be accurately determined. They have remarkably increased the necessary emphasis upon home defence. They have made clearer than ever the tremendous importance of our eastern Atlantic ports for the convoying of military and other supplies to Britain and France.

They have been responsible for the great significance it has been necessary to attach to air development—not only in connection with our own Royal Canadian Air Force, but also in regard to the Commonwealth Air Training Plan, in which we have such a vital part and place.

When you examine the expenditures made, and learn the appropriations proposed, in connection with the Royal Canadian Navy and the Air Force, you will be more than ever impressed by the differences between the waging of war in 1914 and the waging of war in 1940.

The world, perhaps, and Canada with it, has been slow to appreciate the extent and the meaning of these changes.

When we consider, also, the difference in the alignment of forces in this war, the possibilities of the spread of conflict in all directions of the compass, and our national duties for defence and co-operation with our allies not only on our eastern shores but in the Pacific as well, you will have some idea of the manner

in which Canadian defence problems have been enlarged and intensified.

I shall proceed now, Mr. Speaker, to a brief review
of what has been done and planned to date. I shall give
the bare, plain facts in brief outline. Full details will
be supplied by my colleagues as the session continues.

WAR SUPPLY

In connection with supply, the total contracts let to
the 15th day of May, amounted to $275,000,000. Of
these amounts, $200,000,000 have been placed on behalf
of the government of Canada, and $75,000,000 on be-
half of the allied governments. With the exception of
amounts totalling about $50,000,000, all contracts have
been let in Canada.

Twenty shipyards are engaged in the production of
90 vessels of war. Production is well in advance of the
scheduled time. There are under construction 82 aerodromes, 175 construction projects including coastal
fortifications, submarine defences and hangars. There
are on order 9,000 motor vehicles, at a cost of
$14,000,000, 3,000 of which have already been delivered
overseas.

War munitions are being manufactured at a cost of
$80,000,000.

One large explosive plant is under construction. A
second is in the course of organization.

Industry is working at full speed to meet the future
requirements of clothing, boots and personal equipment. The production of small arms munitions is being
expanded as rapidly as equipment can be installed.

The Department of Munitions and Supply, with the
assistance of the War-Time Prices and Trade Board,

has taken every available step to protect sources of outside supply, and ensure against a shortage of raw materials. In addition to this, constant study is given to the possibilities of the increased use of Canadian materials in the production of supplies for ourselves and our allies.

CANADA'S ARMED FORCES

As at May 10, 1940, the personnel of the Royal Canadian Navy consisted of 952 officers, 5,662 ratings. These numbers include 125 Canadian officers and 100 ratings who are serving in the British navy. That personnel is being increased by recruitment, and will be increased as rapidly as ships come into service.

In addition to our 7 destroyers, we have in commission 15 mine-sweepers, 6 anti-submarine vessels, 15 fishermen's reserve vessels, and 51 other auxiliary vessels. The conversion of 3 high-speed merchant ships to light cruisers will be completed shortly.

The Royal Canadian Navy, apart from its patrol duties on our own coasts, is assisting actively in the coastal defence of Newfoundland, and is co-operating with the British and French navies in the Caribbean area. It is also taking an active and important share in the convoy duty so essential if the military supplies and foodstuffs required by the allies are to cross the ocean in security.

In the Royal Canadian Air Force on May 10 of the year, we had 1,389 officers, 10,926 airmen, or 12,315 of all ranks.

In the Canadian active service force, the personnel as at the 10th of May, 1940, was as follows: The first division is overseas, and its strength has been enlarged by the necessary ancillary troops. The number of troops in the first division and its ancillaries is 23,438. At Canadian military headquarters there are 240 officers and men. The total of men overseas is therefore 23,678.

We have in training for overseas service a second division with its ancillary troops amounting to 24,645.

The total personnel in the Canadian active service force as of May 10 is 81,519. Apart from troops overseas and troops engaged in home defence our troops are assisting in the defence of strategic areas in Newfoundland, and further assignments of duties are contemplated in the Atlantic area. In the three services there were as of May 10 more than 100,000 men on active service.

The British Commonwealth Air Training Plan

The British Commonwealth Air Training Plan is not an exclusively Canadian undertaking. As the name implies, it is a joint plan in which the four governments, those of the United Kingdom, Canada, Australia and New Zealand, are all concerned. The Plan originated with the British Government. The preliminary work on the scheme was done by the United Kingdom air ministry. Canada cannot alter the Plan at her own exclusive discretion, nor without regard for the essential factors of the adequate training of men to meet the demands of modern aerial warfare.

I am aware that a growing feeling of impatience has become manifest in certain sections of the country with reference to what is believed to be the slow progress made by the British Commonwealth Air Training Plan and the fact that its contribution is not one of immediate effectiveness at this critical hour. We recognize that these sentiments spring from a very natural desire to carry at this moment a greater share of the load which is being carried by the mother country and our allies across the seas. But we do believe that they are perhaps coloured by lack of understanding of the magnitude of this undertaking, and particularly of the objectives which it is called upon to fulfil. If such a misunderstanding exists it is probably due to the fact that the public has not gained a full appreciation of the size of this project, the greatest individual effort which this dominion has ever made.

ADDITIONAL MINISTRIES AND MEASURES

In order that Canada's contribution in this branch of our war effort may be made as complete and as expeditious as possible, the government has decided to ask parliament to make provision for the appointment of an additional Minister of the Crown to be known as Minister of National Defence for Air, who will give his undivided time and attention to air activities and in particular to a close supervision of the Commonwealth Air Training Plan.

The dynamic forces which have changed the war situation in Europe within recent days; the unprecedented threat to the allied powers and ourselves, must be met at once by immediate action. Production must be accelerated to its limit. Training must be intensified. But however imperative the need, once we have determined—as we have—to meet actual and threatened events to the utmost of our strength and capacity, we must see to it that what is done shall be efficient, persistent and designed to guarantee that action which we believe will contribute most to the defence and triumph of the allied cause. The government proposes that there shall be devoted to the Department of Munitions and Supply the sole, exclusive and full-time services of a Minister of the Crown. His responsibility will be to correlate production activities, and to speed up in every manner possible the output of essential military and other material. For this purpose there will be conferred upon the Department of Munitions and Supply certain special powers which would not be accorded in normal times, to enable it to expedite the provision of equipment of materials of war for the armed forces.

The government has reiterated to the government of the United Kingdom its confidence in the productive capacity of Canadian plants as an alternative source of supply, relatively free from the danger of any enemy action. Canadian manufacturers have expressed their readiness to undertake to the limit of their capacity the production of all such supplies as can be manufactured in this country. The government has undertaken to assist in the organization of the fullest use of the resources of Canadian industry, as and when the British Government indicates its wishes.

To turn to another phase of the matter, the government has taken all possible steps to prevent sabotage and subversive activity, by propaganda or otherwise, against the allied cause. Our efficient Royal Canadian Mounted Police and other branches of the government concerned are fully aware of the situation, and have taken action wherever warranted. I wish, however, in this connection, to make two appeals. I appeal to all citizens of foreign extraction to remember that they are living in a land which is fighting to maintain the freedom which they now enjoy, and the possibilities of international good will which enabled them to settle in our midst. I appeal, also, to all members of the public to refrain from persecution and panic action against harmless and law-abiding people who share our life and, in most instances, our common citizenship.

Canada's Armed Forces Strengthened

In view of the critical turn of events in Europe within the last few days, and in the light of information obtained by the Minister of National Defence on his recent visit to England, the government has decided to take the following additional measures to strengthen our armed forces, and to enlarge our contribution to the allied cause. These decisions, and those which I have already mentioned, are being translated into action. They are all in addition to the work which has been done and planned in the military, naval and air spheres of action, and on the economic front.

We have decided to advance the date of the dispatch overseas of the second division on the Canadian active service force.

We have decided to advance the date of the dispatch of such further re-inforcements of the first division as have not already proceeded overseas.

We have decided to push forward the recruiting of re-inforcements for the second division of the Canadian active service force, which will follow that division overseas at the earliest possible date.

There will be formed a Canadian corps in the field in accordance with arrangements which have been discussed with the British War Office.

Besides the two divisions and their ancillary units, the corps will include the necessary additional corps troops and will involve the dispatch overseas of several thousand men beyond those which I have already mentioned.

We shall undertake the raising of a third division, to be available for such service as may be required in Canada or overseas.

We have assigned, at the request of the United Kingdom Government, certain naval and military formations to active duty in the Caribbean and North Atlantic areas.

There will be dispatched overseas, as soon as possible, No. 112 army co-operation squadron to act as a reserve for No. 110 co-operation squadron now overseas.

As already mentioned, we shall adopt every feasible method of accelerating the output of pilots and air crews from Canada for service in the field, at the earliest possible date.

Steps have been taken in order to advance beyond the agreed and predetermined schedule the preparation of aerodromes, hangars, and training establishments.

ALL ASPECTS OF WORLD SITUATION TO BE KEPT IN MIND

With a world situation such as our own and other countries must face to-day, it is necessary for the government to take account not only of the happenings of the immediate moment but of possible happenings during the period through which this war may run. The situation is vastly different from what it has been heretofore. As I said in my remarks at the outset, during the last war we had Japan as an ally, we had Russia as an ally, we had Italy as an ally and we had practically no problem on the Pacific coast. For some considerable time the United States also was an active ally.

In connection with the Atlantic coast there was very little to be considered. At that time the British navy undertook the protection of our Atlantic coast and we were actually being protected by the British navy in our immediate coastal waters. Our navy was a tiny affair, I believe of two ships, the *Rainbow* and the *Niobe*. These ships were taken over by the British navy and became part of that navy. In this war our navy is a unit which is serving actively on the Atlantic and it is rendering most valuable assistance to the British navy itself.

We know the developments in the war up to date, but we do not know what they are going to be to-morrow. We do not know what they are going to be a week or a month or a year hence. We have, therefore, to consider not only what we can do in the way of co-operation overseas but also the possible happenings with respect to Canada itself. This is one of the things that I hope hon. members will keep in mind. We have to see around all the sides of this situation and view it in relation not only to the Canada that we knew in the last war but to the Canada that is a nation to-day.

One hardly dares to suggest the thought, but should our enemy triumph in this particular struggle it is not

France, it is not England, it is not Holland, it is not Belgium, it is not Norway, it is not Poland and it is not Czechoslovakia that they would seek as a prize of war; what the enemy are looking for are great new areas of development. That is what underlies this struggle for world domination and we cannot afford to ignore at this time every conceivable possibility with relation to each part of the British Commonwealth of Nations.

I need scarcely say that hysteria and panic will add nothing but confusion to the performance of a task that is long and difficult. Munitions and implements of war cannot be forged overnight. The duration and intensity of war have alike to be taken into account. Similarly, the sailors, soldiers and airmen required to meet fresh situations as they arise in all quarters of the globe cannot all be trained at once. No one is more conscious than my colleagues and I of the necessity of vigour of action, patience of heart, and steadfastness of soul. We have acted and shall continue to act to the limit of our wisdom and knowledge and power.

NEW SITUATIONS AND
RESPONSIBILITIES

The amazing rapidity of the German advance in Western Europe and the growing hostility of the Italian Government were the significant features of the war in the months of May and June, 1940. On June 7, the Prime Minister again reviewed the situation in Europe, and gave a further account of Canada's contribution to the war effort of the allied powers. In this broadcast the new responsibilities thrown upon Canada by the development of hostilities were strongly stressed.

NEW SITUATIONS AND RESPONSIBILITIES

BROADCAST, JUNE 7, 1940

I SPEAK to you to-night in the midst of the most crowded weeks in human history. Barely a month has passed since Holland and Belgium were first ravaged by lightning warfare in all its fury and frightfulness. Every succeeding day since their first heroic resistance has brought new shocks, new problems, and new duties to those in whose hands has been placed the task of defending freedom.

The brutal domination of Holland, the tragic surrender of Belgium, the invasion of France, the capture of the channel ports, have happened in such quick succession that the world has hardly had time to breathe. To-day, Britain, no longer in island security, prepares to meet the invader across the narrow sea. At this very hour, the greatest of all battles in history is being waged within 70 miles of the city of Paris. On its outcome may depend the future of France.

As the world has been shaken to its foundations by the swift march of terrible events, nearly every emotion in the heart of each one of us has been profoundly stirred. Hate for the inhuman oppressor, pity for the helpless and the homeless, pride for the brotherhood of the brave who have honoured the lands of Britain and France that gave them birth.

One crisis has not passed before another has arisen in its place. Peril has been heaped upon peril. Who

105

will say on what new horizon destruction may not loom to-morrow?

Three Distinct Periods—I. The Shadow of War

To help you gain a true perspective, may I remind you that the war itself did not commence until September last. Nine months have not yet passed since parliament authorized expenditures for active participation in the war, and in particular for co-operation by Canada with the allied powers in the theatres of war in Europe.

As regards the war, there are three periods which may be considered as separate and distinct. There was the first period, what I might call the shadow of war, during which time there was still a hope for peace. Within that period the democratic nations worked for peace. While they worked for peace, they also prepared for war. If they had not worked for peace, they would have been accused of precipitating war, not only by the present enemies of democracy, but also by their own people. They prepared for war more slowly and later than their enemies. The very strength of democracy in peace-time became in some measure a handicap in war-time, and in preparations for war-time. The final preparations had necessarily to await the hour that would gain for them the sanction of their parliaments. That hour came to Canada with the calling of the special session of our parliament.

II. The Outbreak and Beginnings of War

There begins the second period. When the shadow had deepened, the storm broke and war began. Britain and France believed that the war would be long. They still believe that they were right in that belief. They planned for at least a three-year war; four years were mentioned as a possibility. Hitler doubtless knows that he can only win a short war. Britain and France knew that they could only win a long war. They asked us to join with them in planning for a long war. Our first effort, therefore, while designed to make the greatest possible contribution at the beginning, was also planned so that, from month to month, man-power would grow, production would grow, output of munitions and supplies would grow, until at the critical time when accumulated strength became the decisive factor, it would be available to ensure victory.

III. The Blitzkreig—Lightning War

The third period is that of the blitzkrieg—lightning war, as it is expressed in English. It accords with the plan which Hitler has all along had in mind. Save by those possessed of gangster instincts, its possibility could never have been conceived. It aims to bring, one by one, under the iron heel of Nazi Germany, nation after nation, whether neutral or belligerent, by methods of terrorism and barbarism, unparalleled in warfare throughout the ages. The element of surprise is all-important. The process was under way before the invasion of Poland. It began with the invasion of Austria and Czechoslovakia. It resulted in the destruction of Poland; it has been only too manifest in the conquest of Denmark and Norway, of Holland and Belgium. It is now seeking by lightning strokes to conquer France and Britain.

These two countries have been taken by surprise; not so much by sudden attack upon themselves—sudden attack was expected at the commencement of the war. The surprise has come by the swiftness, the magnitude and the ferocity of the events that preceded them. No part of the world has been shocked by these tragic happenings more than this continent. The loyalty of neutral nations to international law became the weapon with which a treacherous enemy struck at their hearts. They have been sacrificed on the altar of their own neutrality.

An Altered and Much Needed Perspective

The lightning war in Europe has forced Britain and France to view the whole situation in a different perspective. Their plans, and with them, our plans, have had to be changed, and quickened in the light of new and appalling developments. Contributions of men, machines and material have had to be hastened. Daily improvisations have become necessary and have been made. The movements of men and ships have had to be altered. Large additional sums of money have had to be found.

It is, I fear, only too true that the magnitude and speed of action, the immensity of the changes in the military situation, and the unparalleled horrors of the conflict have all but destroyed our sense of time. It is difficult to realize that a month has not yet elapsed since Holland and Belgium were invaded. The heroic resistance of these small nations to the German onslaught, and the magnificent response of Britain and France to their appeal for aid were absorbing the attention of the people of Canada when, just a week later, our new parliament met.

As we watched the spectacle of the German forces

crushing Holland and Belgium under the full might of concentrated warfare, it was inevitable that an unparalleled intensity of feeling should develop throughout the country. There developed equally naturally a tendency to measure our Canadian war effort in terms, not of long-range and carefully laid plans, but in terms of the terrible emergency of the moment. The unexpected rapidity with which the Nazi forces carried out their destructive advance naturally increased the tension and added to an impatient if natural desire for additional immediate action.

CANADA'S WAR EFFORT OBSCURED BY EVENTS

The dramatic events in Europe served to obscure what Canada had done, and was doing to prosecute the war; they also enhanced the difficulty of presenting to parliament and the people a clear picture of our war effort.

As was to be expected, there was an insistent demand that the government should "speed up" its war effort to meet the new situation. At that very time, the government itself was throwing its full energy into adapting our organization and adjusting our plans to conform to the swiftly changing scene in Europe. It was impossible to decide upon changes of plans until accurate information could be secured from the battle front. When decisions were reached, some of them, for military reasons, could not be announced immediately. Some have not been, and can not yet be made public.

I should like to stress that everything that has been done recently has been accomplished in the time it has because the foundations of our war effort were well and truly laid. Many of the measures recently an-

nounced could not have been taken earlier, because the
circumstances did not then call for emergency action
of the character recently undertaken. Terrible risks
must be taken to meet the present crisis—and Canada
is sharing those risks—but we must beware of adding
to necessary risks, the needless risk of abandoning
plans to face a long and bitter struggle in which staying power will, in the end, be decisive. To allow our
passionate feeling to degenerate into unreasoning
hysteria would be fatal to Canada's war effort and a
grave injury to the allied cause.

MEASURES TAKEN TO MEET EMERGENT CONDITIONS

You have heard something in the last few days of
what has been done to meet the terrible emergency.
It could only be disclosed in instalments, and sometimes not at all. Many things must still remain secret.
All disclosures must be made at a time when they suit
the allied needs. I could not tell parliament and
people, for example, of General McNaughton's visit to
the front and of the preparation for our troops to embark for France, until the story of the epic achievement of the evacuation of Dunkirk was made known
to the world. I could not tell of the despatch of our
destroyers to England, until after they had arrived in
British waters. Unfortunately, we have been and still
are often precluded from saying a word of what we
had been asked to do, and of what, in fact, we had done
and are doing.

It may help to bring home to you all a fuller appreciation of what has actually been accomplished if I
summarize some of the results in terms of men, equipment and supply.

I should like, however, first to give you this solemn assurance. We offered to the allies, in the name of the people of Canada, all the additional assistance in our power to help them to deal with the recent emergency. We have made no restrictions. What we could do and have done, what we can produce, what we can manufacture, has been placed at their disposal to the utmost limit of our capacity and strength. They have asked us to do a number of things. We have sought to do each one of them promptly, completely, and without qualification. We have, on our own account, made additional offers and suggestions. Many of them have been accepted.

THE ARMY

In the army, when Belgium and Holland were invaded, we had 81,519 men of all ranks. We had one division, with its ancillary troops, trained and equipped with motorized units on active service in England. 23,000 young Canadians were ready for embarkation to Norway or to Flanders whenever the word came from the Allied High Command.

A second division of men, with necessary auxiliaries, amounting in all to 24,000, were completing their Canadian training.

Strategic areas in Newfoundland were defended by this country's soldiers.

When Hitler's lightning war, the "blitzkrieg", began we advanced the date of the dispatch of our second division. We did likewise with all re-inforcements for the first division, who had not proceeded to England. We speeded the recruiting of re-inforcements for the second division. We undertook the formation of a

Canadian corps in the field and provided the necessary corps troops. We decided to raise a third division. The units have been announced, and recruiting has begun.

We formed a Veterans' Home Guard for the defence of our internal security, and have authorized the establishment of additional veterans' reserves. We undertook to raise rifle battalions for a fourth division. We have established a special training course for officers, and veteran officers.

Canadian soldiers are to-day also on active duty in the West Indies and the North Atlantic.

THE NAVY

In the navy, we began the month of May with 6,614 officers and ratings, including 125 officers and 100 ratings serving in the British navy.

We had 94 vessels in commission.

We had 90 vessels under construction.

Our ships operated on both coasts, in West Indian waters, and convoyed ships from our shores and protected our harbours.

Since the course of the war changed, with the shock of uncontemplated suddenness, we have ordered the recruitment of 4,900 additional men. Every shipyard now works to capacity. And to-day, by one of those strange changes of fate and fortune, our destroyers, willingly repaying a small part of an ancient debt, are helping to guard the shores of Britain, and watch with increasing vigilance for those who would violate her island freedom. I bade them Godspeed when they left with the same pride with which you and the people of Britain greeted their arrival.

Our navy is a young navy. It has inherited great traditions; it is helping to create them.

THE AIR FORCE

The Royal Canadian Air Force had no existence during the last war. At the beginning of May, it had a strength of 12,315 men. We had nine squadrons for home defence, one army co-operation squadron overseas, another completing its training in Canada, and re-inforcements continuously preparing for active service in the Army Co-operation School.

The Commonwealth Air Training Plan was proceeding in magnitude, training, and time in accordance with the predetermined plan.

The Nazis struck with all their power. Their swift advance was made possible by their numerical superiority in the air. We immediately sent overseas No. 112 Army Co-operation Squadron. We called up for immediate service 5,000 recruits for the Royal Canadian Air Force. We undertook to despatch overseas a fighter squadron of the Royal Canadian Air Force. We appointed a Minister to devote his entire time and attention to National Defence for Air.

We have hastened the construction of air fields and hangars a year earlier than the time fixed under the Commonwealth Plan.

We have sent overseas a number of pilots recently graduated from Camp Borden, who were intended to be used as instructors. Many of our own aeroplanes were sent to Britain. Aeroplanes of British manufacture, ordered five months before the outbreak of war, for our own air force, and which in the month of May were on their way out to Canada, were, on our own instructions, stopped in mid-ocean and returned to Britain.

It has been stated that the Commonwealth Air Training Plan will be abandoned or postponed because of these changes. This is not true. It will yet be a decisive instrument of victory.

MONEY AND MATERIALS

Of money, I will say no more than that the present appropriation for war purposes alone is $2,000,000 a day, an amount which will necessarily be increased as we continue to seek to meet exceptional needs.

WAR SUPPLY

By the 10th of May, when the "blitzkrieg" began, orders had been placed for $225,000,000 worth of equipment, material and munitions for the Canadian army, navy and air force. The purchases ranged from clothing and personal equipment to aircraft and ships. Every shipyard in Canada was working at full capacity. The textile and clothing industries were also fully occupied. The production of munitions was being rapidly expanded, and aircraft production was rising steadily.

The blitzkrieg has created new problems of supply. Plans made in the early months of the war provided for the production by Canada of certain lines of equipment and by Britain of others, each to meet the needs of the other in certain respects. Changed circumstances have made it necessary for Canada to produce many things, even at greater cost, which it was expected would be supplied by Britain. In some cases it has been necessary to abandon the practice of using

British specifications, if production is to be carried on speedily enough to meet emergent needs. The Department of Munitions and Supply is grappling vigorously with the new problems.

NEED FOR CONFIDENCE AND CALM

I have told you these things because it is difficult, amid all the news and distractions of war, for anyone in Canada to obtain a clear picture at one time of what is being done to meet the situation.

The government is devoting all its energy, and marshalling all resources to meet the threat to our liberty. We need your confidence. We need the constructive help of every Canadian. In steadfastness and courage remains the hope of human liberty. Panic, dissension, disunity are the only enemies that can defeat us. All is not dark in the skies above us. The first series of enemy gains will not end this war, any more than it ended other wars in which the British and French peoples have fought side by side. The enemy's tactics, his weapons, his strength are now known. They surprised us. They will not defeat us.

In the light of all that is known of the situation as it is shaping itself in Europe to-day, I feel I would not be doing my full duty at this time, if I did not speak of other dangers which threaten.

OPERATIONS IN NEW THEATRES OF WAR

I began by distinguishing three phases of the war. It is difficult to believe that we are not at this moment at the beginning of the fourth phase. Our attention from the outset has been directed to Germany as the sole enemy, and to her effort to destroy Britain and

France. The coming phase will witness operations in entirely new theatres of war. It will most certainly be marked by conflict between nations that thus far have escaped or avoided hostilities. How sudden or how extensive these new developments may be, no one can say. What I wish to make clear is, that if at any moment we learn that fresh hostilities have broken out, on however terrible a scale, there is no reason why fresh fears should occasion undue alarm. We shall have, of course, to assess anew what may be necessary on our part to meet the demand of the new situation. New events will demand new measures, but we will do well to continue to keep the situation as a whole in its perspective.

While not underestimating the dangers that threaten from other coasts and other seas, let us remember that against the perils of the present and the future are arrayed a new realization on the part of all free peoples of the nature of the conflict, and a new determination to spare no effort and no sacrifice in the indomitable will to conquer. If democracy lacked foresight and audacity in the past, those days are over.

New Factors and Friends

The German territorial advances contain within themselves elements of weakness. Economic blockade and contraband control can, and will now be exercised with increasing and more effective pressure. Disregard for the strength and the ruthlessness of the enemy, lack of preparation to meet the demands of modern mechanized warfare, the suspense of waiting for an enemy who shrinks from no violation of right, and no manifestation of terror, all these things have passed away. Discipline has come to us all, not from without, but from within. Wanton brutality has transformed isolation of outlook, and neutrality of heart, into mere empty words. The treachery that stabbed the neutral nations killed neutrality itself with the same fell blow.

If new enemies oppose us, we may be sure that old and new friends will arise to help us. The world-wide significance of the conflict is being realized in every land. You know how earnestly and vigorously the President of the United States has spoken in the name of humanity. There has been mobilized in the cause of freedom, the conscience of the civilized world, and tyranny will long remember the power of that conscience, and the final effect of the world's condemnation upon the forces of evil.

CANADA'S NEW RESPONSIBILITY

Canada is called upon to accept a greater and higher responsibility. It was framed in living words by Mr. Churchill in his speech to the British House of Commons on Tuesday last. This nation with all the strength of its youth, the wealth of its resources, and the idealism of its freedom, will proudly accept its new responsibility. We are the bridge between the old world and the new; the bridge which joins the new freedom of the North American continent with the ancient freedom of Britain which gave it birth. We will stand resolute to defend its approaches and its abutments.

From the harbour of Dunkirk and from the citadel of Calais the bravest men in the world battled their way home to fight once again for liberty and goodness and mercy.

To the making of Canada have come the same chivalry of France and the same gallantry of Britain which fashioned the glory of that triumph of heroism. I speak the heart and mind of our country when I say that every fort in Canada will be another Calais, and every harbour will be another Dunkirk, before the men and women of our land allow the light and the life of their Christian faith to be extinguished by the powers of evil, or yield their liberties to the tyranny of Nazi brutality.

ITALY ENTERS THE WAR

On June 10th Italy declared her intention to enter the war on the side of Germany. By unanimous resolution of the Commons and Senate, Canada's entry into a state of war with Italy was approved. On the same day a state of war between Canada and Italy was officially proclaimed.

That evening the Prime Minister in a nationwide broadcast spoke of the situation created by the entry of Italy into the war, and drew attention to the aid about to be given by the United States.

ITALY ENTERS THE WAR

BROADCAST, JUNE 10, 1940

THE NEWS reached Ottawa a few minutes after one o'clock to-day that Signor Mussolini, in a speech delivered at Rome, had announced that Italy was entering the war on the side of Germany. The official confirmation of this news was not received until the House of Commons met this afternoon. Realizing that the people of Canada would wish the government to take action without delay, I immediately introduced a resolution which placed Canada at the side of Britain and France in the war against Italy, as was done with respect to the war against Germany in September last. The same resolution was introduced and unanimously passed. A meeting of the Cabinet was held to-night, an order-in-council was passed, tendering to His Majesty the King the advice that a Proclamation should issue, declaring that a state of war existed between Canada and the Kingdom of Italy as and from June 10, 1940. The terms of the order-in-council were immediately communicated by cable to the Canadian High Commissioner in London, for submission to the King. As soon as His Majesty's approval has been given a Proclamation will be issued in the *Canada Gazette,* similar in form to that of September 10, 1939, which declared that a state of war existed with the German Reich.

The Minister of Justice has authorized the Royal Canadian Mounted Police to take steps to intern all

residents of Italian origin whose activities have given
ground for the belief or reasonable suspicion that they
might, in time of war, endanger the safety of the State,
or engage in activities prejudicial to the prosecution
of the war. Other necessary measures have been taken
to prevent trading with the new enemy, or performing
other acts which are not consistent with a state of war.
Preparations for these and other necessary steps had
been made well in advance of the declaration of war.

ITALY'S TREACHERY FORESEEN

When I spoke to you on Friday evening last, I told
you that before many days would pass there was every
likelihood that nations which had hitherto avoided or
escaped warfare would engage in hostilities. The signs
were there for all to see, and messages from Europe
served only to confirm the foreboding. As foreseen at
that time and as I stated this afternoon in the House
of Commons, after many months of preparation, provocation in act and word and threat of open hostility,
Italy has thrown her resources into the war at the side
of Nazi Germany.

The motives that have inspired the government of
Italy, and the methods which Italy has pursued are
well known. With a callousness and treachery second
only to that of Hitler, the German dictator, Mussolini,
the dictator who holds the Italian people in thrall, has
chosen what he believes to be the psychological moment to strike at Britain and France in the Mediterranean and Africa in order to satiate his lust for conquest and territorial aggrandizement, and for such
glory as calculated duplicity and treachery can bring.

Betrayal of an Ancient Friendship

Barely eighty years ago, the peoples of Italy passed from serfdom and disunion to liberty and unity. In the struggles which are imperishably associated with the names of Mazzini, Cavour and Garibaldi, the English-speaking peoples gave to the Italian people a moral and material support that contributed in no small measure to the establishment and preservation of the Italian nation. At a time when the rest of Europe looked with eyes of apathy, and even of hostility, upon the rebirth of Italy, the government of the United Kingdom in a memorable dispatch advised the Italian people that they turned their sympathetic eyes to the gratifying prospect of a people building up the edifice of their liberties, and consolidating the work of their independence. The shouts of welcome of the British people to Garibaldi still ring through the years. As his great English biographer said:

"Garibaldi will live as the incarnate symbol of two passions not likely soon to die out of the world, of love of country, and the love of freedom kept pure by the one thing that can tame and yet not weaken them, the tenderest humanity for all mankind."

Italy grew in power and in influence amidst many evidences of good will from those who had hailed her rise to nationhood. Her citizens were welcomed in all the lands of the British Commonwealth beyond the seas, and not least in Canada. In the last Great War, she shared with us the burden of the day. She was rewarded with some of the fruits of victory. Through many generations, Britain and France and their sons and daughters have turned to the art and literature of Italy for solace and inspiration. To countless millions her capital city has been one of the holy places of the world. From Rome, the spiritual power and comfort of an ancient and undying faith have gone into the lands of all the earth.

Amidst the discord and clamour of a world which is falling in ruins around us, I do not forget at this time the noble example set by the present occupant of the Holy See in his unceasing work for the preservation of peace and the exaltation of humanity itself.

All these ancient traditions of freedom and good will, of religion, of literature and of art have been trampled upon and cast by wicked men into the darkness and dust.

THE STRENGTH AND WEAKNESS OF ITALY

It would be a great mistake to underestimate the seriousness of the new situation which has been created. Italy is a nation of forty millions. Under the domination of her dictator, she has been preparing for war longer than any other nation in Europe. A whole generation has been educated to glorify force. It is useless further at this time to regret the degradation of a free and peaceful people, to seek the causes for the change, or to condemn the evil doctrines which have poisoned the hearts and minds of Italian youth. The very names of Ethiopia and Albania are reminders of the use of overwhelming force to subdue the weak.

While at the moment the allied world breathes harder, it may truly be said that it breathes more easily. The suspense of the Italian threat has now been removed. It has become a stark reality. The addition of Italian strength to the enemy will need redoubled energy and increased determination on the part of us all. We know where Italy stands. The atmosphere is cleared. The hands of Britain and France are freed for immediate and vigorous action.

The spread of ruthless warfare into other seas, and on other shores, may well have an incalculable effect upon the opinion and attitude of those who still call themselves neutral. While Italy has it in her power to occasion much damage and to divert the allied effort from the main task of defeating Germany she is herself particularly vulnerable on both the military and economic fronts of the conflict and cannot for long hope to stand the strain of war.

Mussolini's Action the Most Ignoble in History

History will, I believe, record no action more ignoble than that of Mussolini. During these tragic months he has sat like a carrion bird of prey waiting for brave men to die.

To-day, he has declared war on those who were the traditional friends of his countrymen.

Callously and cynically, he has chosen what he believes is the fateful hour for the swoop and the treacherous blow.

Peaceful overtures, proffered concessions, bonds of ancient friendship sealed by the memory of common sacrifices in the cause of freedom, all these he has bartered for the vision of conquest and the phantom of power.

No one can foretell the horror that the spread of warfare in lands hitherto untouched by its ravages may bring to the world. But one thing is sure. Retribution will overtake all tyrants and the dictator of

Italy amongst them. It is too early to predict the final effect of this treachery upon those who cannot sit idly by and watch the whole world become gradually but inexorably engulfed in the seas of battle. We may rest assured that the forces of liberty will rally in a supreme effort of victory.

An Old Friend and a New Friend

When I spoke to you on Friday, I used these words:

"If new enemies oppose us, we may be sure that old and new friends will rise to help us."

Many of you no doubt heard to-night the eloquent voice of both an old and a new friend—President Roosevelt. An old friend, because his heart, and the hearts of his people have always beaten in sympathy with ours. A new friend because in his ringing declaration, he pledged the material resources of his great and powerful country to strengthen and maintain the cause of freedom.

As for Canada this new peril to the allied cause will only increase our country's determination to stand resolutely at the side of Britain and France until the powers of evil which threaten the freedom of mankind are vanquished once and for all.

CANADA'S WAR ADMINISTRATION

His Excellency The Right Honourable The Earl of Athlone assumed office as Governor-General of Canada upon his arrival in Ottawa on June 21. Among measures assented to by His Excellency on the day of his arrival was the National Resources Mobilization bill. Under this statute, all the resources of the nation, both human and material, were placed at the disposal of the State for the prosecution of the war.

The determination of war policy and the direction of the war effort had been entrusted by the Cabinet to a War Committee of the Cabinet which was formed shortly after Canada entered the war. The responsibilities assumed by Canada necessitated, as the war effort developed, a progressive enlargement of the powers and the administrative machinery of the government.

An outline of the administrative developments was given to the House of Commons by the Prime Minister on July 8, 1940. The Prime Minister also spoke of considerations governing membership in the Cabinet. As a means of increasing public confidence in Canada's war effort, an invitation was extended to the Leader of the Opposition and to the leaders of other parliamentary groups in the House of Commons to become associate members of the War Committee of the Cabinet, or to unite, at regular intervals, in conference with its members. Neither of these proposals, however, was accepted.

CANADA'S WAR ADMINISTRATION

C ANADA's war effort has been, from the first, and will continue to be organized and directed by the Cabinet. From the outset, the work of the Cabinet has been so organized as to permit of immediate and effective direction of the various activities, and at the same time to ensure their complete co-ordination. For the most effective conduct of that effort, the Cabinet itself has been organized into appropriate committees, each charged with responsibilities in specific spheres of activity.

As a supervisory body in a position to view the war effort as a whole, an Emergency Council was appointed with an immediate relationship to the work of the several governmental committees. At the outset, this Emergency Council was composed of senior members of the Cabinet. Amongst other duties, it took over those of the Defence Committee established prior to the war. As occasion has since required, its personnel has been altered or increased to include the Ministers whose departments are specially concerned with the war effort. In an early reorganization, its name was changed. It has since been designated and is now known as the War Committee of the Cabinet. The War Committee of the Cabinet gives continuous consideration to major questions of war policy and defence.

The need for the expansion of administrative per-

sonnel was more urgent at the outbreak of war than the
need for the expansion of the Cabinet. The need, however, of creating new Ministries to meet war-time demands, and of assigning to their administration, Ministers whose time could be exclusively devoted to the
supervision and encouragement of their affairs has
become only too obvious. Existing Ministries have accordingly been enlarged. New Ministries have been
established, and yet further Ministries concerned exclusively with war-time activities are about to be
created. To offset this expansion of war-time services,
the activities of peace-time services have been materially curtailed.

CONSIDERATIONS GOVERNING CABINET RECONSTRUCTION

The filling of Cabinet posts is a more complicated
task than the filling of administrative posts. Ability
to direct the work of the government departments concerned is, of course, an important requisite. It is,
however, far from being the only one. A Cabinet
Minister must also be prepared to assume his full
share of responsibility for all acts of government, and
for explaining the policies of the government to parliament and to the country. He must, of course, be a
Member of Parliament. If he is not in parliament
when he is called to the Cabinet he must find a con-
stituency and be elected in it. Above all he must have
a capacity to work in immediate association with other
Ministers in the Cabinet in the formulation of policy.
Nothing would paralyze government more quickly than
divided counsels or dissension within the Ministry.

That does not mean that narrow party consideration governs the choice of Ministers, particularly in

war-time. But it does mean that different qualities are required for effective work as a Cabinet Minister from those required in an administrative or executive post. It is a common experience to find that a business man is willing to make very great personal sacrifice in order to serve his country in an administrative capacity, but is exceedingly reluctant to enter the Cabinet because a ministerial post involves election to parliament, public speaking and other activities for which he feels he has neither aptitude nor training.

Furthermore, the acceptance of a Cabinet post involves a more complete severance of business and professional ties than is necessary in undertaking temporary administrative or advisory appointments. There is no business of any magnitude or importance in this country to which the war has not brought particular problems of its own. Highly placed executives may be spared by such concerns either in an executive or advisory capacity, for whole or part-time, without the risks attendant upon a complete severance of business relations such as would be involved in their entering the Ministry.

PARLIAMENTARY EXPERIENCE AN ALL-IMPORTANT FACTOR

It is an open secret that I have directly and indirectly offered to take into the Ministry outstanding persons, none of whom are at present in public life, but whose presence in the Ministry would, I believe, have made wholly apparent the readiness of my colleagues and myself to associate with ourselves in the work of the Ministry persons whose appointment could in no sense be regarded as made from any party political motive, but only on the ground of the outstanding qualities the persons appointed were known to possess.

I have found that those I approached felt that such special services as they could render could be given more effectively, either in administrative posts or in an advisory capacity or by their continuing to occupy an eminent and independent position in the community. The prevalence of this attitude was not the least of the reasons which led me to abandon the attempt to add to the Cabinet from outside the ranks of those without previous experience of public life.

It is sometimes forgotten that the intimacy and prominence of the associations enjoyed with large enterprises are not infrequently a barrier rather than a passport to membership in a Cabinet. The same consideration does not so generally apply where the services to be rendered are not concerned with the determining of policy but with its execution.

I have come to the conclusion that, for the present at least, the most effective use can be made of the services of men without previous experience of public life by bringing them into association with the Ministry in an administrative or advisory capacity rather than by their inclusion in the Ministry itself.

Opposition Invited to Have Associate Members of War Committee

Realizing the importance of increasing public confidence through bringing to the aid of the Ministry all points of view and opinions, I have considered yet another means by which this end might possibly be attained. I have thought of inviting leading members of the Opposition to become Associate Members of the War Committee of the Cabinet, to share its

deliberations and to assist in the formation of its proposals to the Cabinet. Regardless of what course may
be adopted, the government itself must, in the last
analysis, take the responsibility for whatever is done
or left undone. That responsibility cannot be escaped
or evaded. It is difficult even to share it. It would not
be my idea, in case members of the Opposition became
Associate Members of the War Committee of the
Cabinet, for the government by that means to seek
in any way to evade full and final responsibility for
Canada's war effort.

But the presence in an advisory and associate capacity of members of the Opposition would have a
number of advantages. While their addition to the
War Cabinet would leave unimpaired the requirements
of responsible government, it would mean that the
government's policies were being shaped and made
effective not only under the open gaze of members of
the Opposition, but with the assistance of their counsel,
experience and advice. It would mean that in all major
matters of defence, internal security, international co-
operation, the leading members of the Opposition,
chosen to act in association with members of the War
Cabinet, would be fully informed.

At the present time, one of the great difficulties of
government lies in the fact that many matters of which
the government has knowledge, many steps which the
government takes, many actions which the government
plans, are, in the very nature of things, highly confidential, and must remain so for varying periods of
time. This obstacle would, in part at least, be over-
come by the proposed Associate Membership of Opposition Leaders in the War Committee of the Cabinet,

where, to its members, their experience, advice and point of view would certainly be of value. I believe that such a step would be of real assistance to the government in the discharge of its great responsibilities. I am therefore prepared to invite the Leader of the Opposition (Mr. Hanson), and the hon. member for Yale (Mr. Stirling), who shares his desk, and was a former Minister of National Defence, to become Associate Members of the War Committee of the Cabinet. Were the invitation accepted, it would be my wish that they should be present at all meetings of the War Committee and take part in all its proceedings. I am prepared also, if this invitation is accepted by hon. friends opposite, and if it is agreeable to other political groups in the house, to consider the extension of the invitation also to their leaders.

If the house and the gentlemen whom I have invited look upon the proposal with favour, it would mean that the country would have the benefit of their wisdom, advice and experience, but the government would retain the responsibility for the direction of Canada's war effort, with which it has been charged. It would also be understood that members of the various opposition groups in this house would continue to be free to criticize the administration as they think fit, and to vote and act with complete independence.

Conferences With Opposition Proposed

If the hon. gentlemen opposite should feel that they were unable to accept the invitation I have just extended, believing that thereby they would be accepting a share of responsibility without being accorded an equivalent share of power, I am prepared to make yet another proposal, the acceptance of which, I should hope, would not occasion the slightest embarrassment and which I feel would be essentially helpful at this time.

As I have already said, much of the action of the government and even more of the information on which its actions are based must, for military reasons, remain secret. This consideration hampers the government in the discussion of its policies and action in parliament and before the people. We recognize that it is an even more serious embarrassment to those in Opposition in war-time. Their lack of knowledge makes effective criticism difficult; it has also a tendency to breed misgivings which need not exist if the facts could be made available. I believe that this situation could be remedied at least in part while parliament is in session by regular weekly conferences between the War Committee and the members of the Opposition and by similar conferences held at intervals when parliament is not in session.

At such conferences the government would be prepared to disclose, in confidence, full and detailed information both as to its actions and the considerations on which those actions are based. The effectiveness of the Opposition, far from being impaired, will be greatly increased by the knowledge gained by their leaders by such conferences. Members of the Opposition, as regards their rights of criticism, will have, as they have now, only the limits imposed by their personal sense of responsibility as citizens and Members of Parliament. From the standpoint of the public interest conferences of this kind would certainly have the merit of increasing confidence in Canada's war effort and thereby help to prevent the development of uneasiness which provides such a fertile ground for subtle enemy propaganda aimed at destroying the unity of that effort.

MAINTENANCE OF RESPONSIBLE GOVERNMENT

I have offered to gentlemen opposite, in the only manner I have felt consistent with responsible government, an opportunity to share in our deliberations. By that invitation I have asked them also to give to the government the benefit of their wisdom and their experience. I have not asked them to share in our ultimate responsibilities because that would not be fair either to them or to the electors of this country.

I hope that my honourable friends will find themselves able to accept one or other of the proposals I have made. Whatever may be their decision I believe that I can at least make this claim on behalf of my colleagues and myself. We have not flinched from our primary and ultimate responsibility. We have not trimmed our sails to the breezes of popular favour or disfavour. While we have recognized our responsibility for policy, we have sought to obtain the best advice available in the country to assist us in its formation and pronouncement.

I leave this recital of facts with confidence to this house and the people of Canada. It tells its own story. It is the brief record of a government which, at a time of great peril in the affairs of the world, has done everything in its power to meet its responsibilities, to strengthen its administration, to mobilize the brain-power and resources of this country—in short, to do its plain duty, fully, honourably and fearlessly.

MIDSUMMER 1940—
CANADA'S WAR EFFORT IN REVIEW

Shortly before the adjournment of parliament, which came on August 7, 1940, two days were devoted in the House of Commons to a review of Canada's war effort. The review took the form of reports on the work of their departments by the ministers principally concerned with the direction of the war effort. The series was prefaced on July 29, with an introductory statement by the Prime Minister.

MIDSUMMER 1940—CANADA'S WAR EFFORT IN REVIEW

THE HOUSE OF COMMONS, JULY 29, 1940

THE KALEIDOSCOPIC changes in the war itself have brought changes equally swift and equally colourful in the methods which have been necessary to meet them. Improvisations have had to be fitted into plans. Men have had to be moved to unexpected spheres of action. The production of materials has needed to be enlarged and hastened beyond what were believed to be the necessities of time and extent. Unprecedented measures had to be taken to provide for the requisite financial appropriations. The collapse of neutral and allied countries, the intensity of air warfare, the spread of the conflict to distant lands, circumstances which have sent Canadian soldiers and resources and ships to the West Indies, Newfoundland, Iceland and the seas that wash the shores of the United Kingdom and France—all these things have made it difficult to reduce to a single presentation the panorama of passing events.

It is not easy to see the picture steadily and as a whole. The whole has sometimes been obscured by the parts. The perspective of 1940 has often been lost in the memories of 1914. The Canadian scene has often become almost invisible in the smoke of the battleground of Europe. I hope that as a result of the facts which will be told to the house to-day a clearer picture will emerge in the minds of parliament and the people of Canada. Let me say that the recital of facts which will follow is not intended as a recital of the achievements of a political party. It represents the achievements of the Canadian people, directed by the government and assisted by the constructive criticism of His Majesty's loyal Opposition.

EFFORT IN OUTLINE

May I give a few broad outlines of our war effort. We have had:

First, to organize and expand the defences of Canada on land, on sea and in the air;

Second, to furnish the maximum aid to the common cause in men and machines of war, wherever they were most needed;

Third, to organize the production of machines and munitions of war, so that output shall reach the highest possible maximum and private profits be held at the lowest possible minimum;

Fourth, to organize the production, distribution and transportation of foodstuffs to meet the needs of war;

Fifth, to prevent any undue rise in prices, and to protect the consumers of Canada against manipulation and speculation;

Sixth, to strengthen the nation's financial structure by taxation, by borrowing, and by the stabilization of international exchange;

Seventh, to provide the necessary machinery to mobilize the material and human resources of the country in the national interest, without fear or favour towards any class, section or interest in the country; and to mobilize these resources by progressive stages in a manner which will best serve to enlarge the scope and enhance the effectiveness of our war effort;

Eighth, to make provision for the internal security of the nation against sabotage to industry, transport and other vital services; to guard against hostile propaganda and espionage and other so-called "fifth column" activities; to take precautions against enemy aliens and sympathizers;

Ninth, to assist in providing for the security of Britain through the reception of enemy aliens and prisoners of war for internment in Canada, and for the reception of such children as the British Government is prepared to send to Canada in order to remove them to a place of safety;

Tenth, to correlate national war services and voluntary effort under government direction and to provide appropriate and helpful ways and means of utilizing the essential patriotism of our citizens and their willingness and expressed desire to work for the common cause.

A Remarkable Transformation

To accomplish these ends and to further these purposes it may be said, in a word, that Canada has brought into being, on a scale that is constantly expanding, an army for service overseas and for home defence; has been building and manning a navy which to-day is assisting in the defence of our coasts, in convoying ships across, in patrolling Atlantic waters, and in repelling enemy forces which threaten the invasion of the British Isles; and has organized and established an air force which is in service at home and abroad. We have, moreover, assumed responsibility for the supervisions of the gigantic commonwealth air training plan and have vastly expedited its development. In a word we have, in addition to the measures taken for the immediate defence and security of our own land, sent ships and troops and airmen to the West Indies, to Newfoundland, to Iceland and to Europe. We have made tremendous commitments for the production of machines and munitions.

The review by the ministers of the departments of government more immediately concerned will set forth in detail what has been done and is further planned to fulfil our duty and implement the legislation which parliament has passed.

The record which will be unfolded represents a remarkable transformation of a peace-loving nation of eleven millions into a people unitedly and effectively organized to fight for the preservation of freedom and democracy. It is the record of a people determined, unceasingly and increasingly, to give of their utmost to the cause of human freedom.

LABOUR AND THE WAR

On August 17, the Prime Minister met the President of the United States at Ogdensburg, New York. The outcome of that meeting was the Agreement to establish a Canada-United States Permanent Joint Board on Defence. The Board was constituted within the course of a few days. Colonel O. M. Biggar, K.C., was appointed Chairman of the Canadian section, and Hon. Fiorello H. La Guardia, Mayor of New York, Chairman of the United States section.

September 1, a year to the day from the outbreak of hostilities, being also the eve of Labour Day, the Prime Minister availed himself of the occasion to give a national message to the workers of Canada on the significance of the two anniversaries.

LABOUR AND THE WAR

BROADCAST, SEPTEMBER 1, 1940

THE PLAIN picture of the ordinary man, working with the strength of his arm, and the skill of his hand, to feed, to clothe and to shelter his fellows, has always seemed to me to represent Humanity in one of its noblest aspects. To improve conditions of Labour is to better the human lot on this earth. That, I suppose, is the motive which most of us have closest to our heart when the enthusiasm of young manhood, and the realization of the duties of citizenship, begin to mould our consciences and our conduct. It is one of the tragedies of life that, amid the complexities of the struggle for existence, the enthusiasm and the realizaiton are so often lost. To my mind, the measure of human greatness is the degree to which we continue to hold, to the end of our days, an enthusiasm for human betterment.

Let me then talk to you to-night of this war not only in relation to its broad aspects but in its relation particularly to Labour. Let us consider together what the winning of this war may mean to Labour. Let us ponder what the loss of this war will certainly mean to Labour. Let us think together for a few minutes of what Labour has done, and can do for the winning of the war. In this, throughout, let us face the facts.

A YEAR OF WAR IN REVIEW

At the end of a year, silence and darkness have fallen upon Poland, Denmark, Norway, Belgium, Luxembourg, Holland. We mourn, too, the tragedy of a

145

broken France. With her withdrawal from the conflict, we lost a gallant ally. With the entry of Italy on the side of Germany, we faced another treacherous and rapacious foe. The few nations of the continent of Europe that have not already been subjugated, either tremble or bow before the might and violence of the aggressor.

Fire and slaughter have spread to Africa and the Near East. There is an ominous glow on the horizons of the Middle East. In many parts of the world, the thunder of the storm is heard, even though the lightning has not yet struck. Ships have battled on all the seven seas. From the skies, over the continent of Europe and the British Isles, aerial warfare continues to rain death and destruction. Millions of innocent, peace-loving, plain, ordinary, simple men and women, who have asked nothing more than to live their lives in the quiet of their own homes, and the shelter of their native valleys, have been dispossessed, robbed and enslaved.

The Significance of Labour Day

Let me now speak of another anniversary. To-morrow, Labour in Canada will celebrate in complete freedom a day, which, by Act of Parliament, has been set apart to honour the place which Labour has gained and holds in our national life. It is deeply significant that such a celebration is possible at the end of a year of total war in Europe.

Every Labour Day is a lighthouse of democracy. As its rays revolve, we see beneath them the freedom and the well-being which we have achieved. As its light flashes to-night, we catch a glimpse of the land of our dreams. We can see the Canada we have longed for and worked for, a land in which men and women, regardless of race, creed or class, can live their lives without fear. For we have cherished the realities of freedom which are also its ideals; the right to think, the right to speak, the right to organize, the right to work, the right to worship.

We believe in the right of men to enjoy the fruits of their honest labour. We believe in the sanctity of humanity, and in man's progressive capacity to take upon himself more of the attributes of Divinity. However much we have failed in what we have done, nevertheless, in our innermost hearts, I believe, we have given a "value immeasurable and eternal to the humblest of human lives."

France until recently was of this household of democracy. So also were Denmark, Norway, Holland and Belgium. Within the space of a single year, we have witnessed the extinction of democracy on the continent of Europe. Beyond the confines of the British Commonwealth of Nations and the United States of America, democracy scarcely survives in the world to-day. That is the next great fact which we have now to face.

We have not needed Hitler and Mussolini to tell us that dictatorship is at war with democracy. In a world of narrowing distances, there is no longer room for these two systems to survive side by side. Sooner or later, the one will extinguish the other. Light will fade into darkness or the darkness will vanish before the light. As has so frequently been said, it is just as true of the world to-day as it was of the American

Union in Lincoln's day, that society no longer can continue to exist half-slave and half-free.

EUROPE'S MIDNIGHT HOUR

Recently I re-read the little poem entitled "Abraham Lincoln Walks at Midnight." It seems to me to reflect the tragedy and the hope of this zero hour. It pictures that great figure restless upon his native hillside, contemplating the sickness of the world, the bitterness, the folly, the pain and the black terror that have come upon the homesteads of men. Listen to these words:

"He cannot rest until a spirit-dawn
  Shall come:—the shining hope of Europe free;
  The league of sober folk, the Workers' Earth,
  Bringing long peace to Cornland, Alp and Sea."

Europe has reached that midnight hour. Whether Labour Day in Canada a year hence will witness the spirit-dawn of a Europe free, or the night of Naziism casting its gloom in deepening shadows over this North American continent, will depend upon the strength, the will, and the untiring work, not of one democracy, but of all the democracies that have survived. In their combined effort, no force can be greater than the truth in Labour's heart and the strength of Labour's arm.

If we lack the vision to see the peril, and the strength to meet it, we, on this North American continent, like the nations of Europe, may come to disaster in one of two ways. This continent might be dominated through actual invasion and conquest. On the other hand, if we fail to carry on the struggle in Europe until tyranny is destroyed, disaster will follow no less surely even though not one Nazi soldier were to land upon our shores.

The triumph of the Nazis in Europe would involve, for the peoples of this continent, the substitution of fear for freedom, and of economic domination for social progress. It would spell the doom of democracy in the New World.

In considering the fate of the democracies, there is another grim fact which we must face. It was unthought of a year ago. It bears immediately both on the possibilities of invasion, and upon the perils of competing industrial standards. This fact is that Nazi Germany has added to her own resources those of the countries she has subjugated. She has acquired a vast supply of the materials and equipment of war which, at the outbreak of war, it was expected would never be used at all, or, if they were, would be used against her. All France, as we know, is in the control of the enemy; the whole western seaboard of Europe from Norway to Spain is in German hands. All the ports and airfields of this continental coast line, once in possession of friendly or allied powers, to-day provide the bases from which the enemy pursues his course across the skies and seas. In addition to the resources of their own land and of France, the Nazis have seized and now possess the resources, the equipment, and the manufacturing plants of Austria, Czechoslovakia, Poland, Denmark, Norway, Holland and Belgium.

Great Britain, Canada, and the other nations of the Commonwealth now fight some 120 million Germans and Italians who have acquired resources and control factories far in excess of the resources and factories of their own lands.

As a result of conquering most of the industrial nations of Europe, and smashing their state organiza-

tions, social institutions and trade unions, Hitler has
masses of impoverished men and women numbering
more than 80,000,000 forced by dire need to work for
the lowest possible wages. However unwilling may be
their obedience, however reluctant their contributions
to their Nazi masters, they do represent a powerful
addition to the effective strength of the enemy.

Freedom of Europe Essential to North American Freedom

Canada has become the bridge which joins the new
freedom of the North American continent with the
ancient freedom of Britain. May we not see in the
means now being taken to secure the common interests
of the British Commonwealth and the United States,
not only the surest of the safeguards of democracy,
but a promise of peace and understanding, and an enduring contribution to the cause of freedom in the
world.

Unless Naziism in Europe is destroyed, the threat
of world domination by a ruthless foe will hang continuously over our heads just as, in recent years, the
threat of invasion and domination has hung over the
heads of the free peoples of Europe. To meet that
threat, our own standards of behaviour and living
would increasingly become those of the totalitarian
states. Our democratic institutions, one by one, would
disappear, and with them what we have won of
freedom.

Unless the enemy is defeated and the enslaved countries of Europe restored to freedom, there will be no
prospect of improving or even of maintaining the
standards of Canadian life which Canadian energy and

Canadian skill have won, no hope of enlarging the opportunities for the happiness of our own or succeeding generations. Free labour will have to compete with slave labour. Men who have hitherto had the right to choose where they would work, and at what they would work, will find themselves in hopeless competition with conscript labour, automatic, soulless, driven by the merciless lash of a ruthless state.

Moreover, failure to free the peoples of Europe from their present thraldom, will mean confining within narrowing limits the areas in which the democracies, should they survive, can hope to develop intercourse in trade or friendship. Many of the markets in which the workmen and the producers of the North American continent have sold their goods will certainly disappear. Overseas we will be forced to compete with men who know no standards, and with states that will sacrifice every standard. In a vain effort to maintain our standards, we will be driven to trade almost exclusively with ourselves. As a last impelling alternative, slowly, certainly and inexorably, we too will become conscripts in the regimentation of the state, and the hewers of wood and the drawers of water for the new economic masters of the world.

To Labour, these facts have spoken and will speak with emphasis and conviction. Labour knows the stake in the struggle between dictatorship and democracy. It understands the difference between rule by force by those who seek a monopoly of power, and government by consent for the common good. It knows the difference between men who despise equality, and seek privilege, possessions and power, and those who believe in the brotherhood of man and the Fatherhood of God.

THE TWO GREAT BROTHERHOODS

In war, no work, no effort, can compare with the
sacrifice of the soldier, the sailor and the airman. Their
sacrifice is uppermost in the thoughts of this nation;
it will live in its memories. But Canadians will remember too the debt they owe to labour. In Canada,
Labour has extended its hours, surrendered its holi-
days, and in its determination to increase and advance
production, has taught the young and the inexperi-
enced the intricacies of complicated trades. It will be
the duty of the people of Canada, realizing these things
now, to remember them in the hour of victory.

In the deeds of the men who on land, on sea and in
the air, offer their lives to save us, Labour is the partner and the ally. With labour rests the power to
shorten the duration of war and, thereby, to save mul-
titudes of human lives. Every workman knows that
every bolt, every piece of steel, every bullet, every
machine part fashioned in Canada is a work for victory. Every workman knows that lacking the machines
of war, the bravest men in the world will avail nothing.

A distinguished British journalist who recently
visited Canada, said that he found Canada at war with
Hitler and at peace with herself. We are at war, and
we shall remain united in will and purpose. But we
can only remain at peace with ourselves if shirking no
effort, withholding no wealth, and sparing no sacrifice, we prove ourselves worthy of our two great
brotherhoods—the brotherhood of the brave who fight
for us, and the brotherhood of Labour that works for
their victory.

JAPAN AND THE NEW ORDER

The months between the adjournment of parliament, on August 7, 1940, and its prorogation on November 5, witnessed the first repulse of the enemy in the Battle of Britain. The second session was opened on November 7, and on November 12 the Prime Minister gave parliament a comprehensive review of the international scene.

On September 27, a pact was signed at Berlin by Germany, Italy and Japan, under the terms of which it was agreed that, in certain contingencies, the three axis powers would assist one another with all political, economic and military means.

In his review, the attention of the Members of the House of Commons was drawn, by the Prime Minister, to the role of Japan in the new alliance. The formal recognition by Germany and Italy of Japan's leadership in creating a new order in East Asia was stated to be a part of the subtle method by which, as the ultimate end of aggression, Nazi Germany, under Hitler, hopes to accomplish its aim of world domination.

JAPAN AND THE NEW ORDER

THE HOUSE OF COMMONS, NOVEMBER 12, 1940

THE BATTLE of Britain, the Nazi pressure on the Balkans, the apparent stalemate in Africa, the Italian attack upon Greece have not been the only events on the international scene since parliament adjourned. The axis powers have also sought by diplomacy, propaganda and intrigue to isolate Britain, and to begin a process of piecemeal destruction of her power and possessions. The pact signed by Germany, Italy and Japan at Berlin on September 27 cannot be viewed as other than an instrument to that end. It contains articles providing for recognition of the respective conquests and spheres of influence of these powers—an open avowal of their existing attitudes towards one another. Article 3, however, goes much farther. It provides that the three axis powers will:

" . . . assist one another with all political, economic, and military means, if one of the high contracting parties should be attacked by a power not at present involved in the European war or in the Sino-Japanese conflict."

A subsequent article provides that this commitment does not affect the relations which exist between the three contracting parties and Soviet Russia. Significantly, no mention is made of the United States. The whole agreement, and the publicity given to it, however, are obviously aimed at intimidating the United

155

States. No matter how clear it may be that freedom and the democratic way of life everywhere are bound up with the fate of Britain, the United States is to be prevented from moving any closer to Britain's side.

DEMANDS ON FRENCH INDO-CHINA FORECAST

The role of Japan in the new alliance is particularly significant. Germany and Italy have formally recognized Japanese leadership in creating a "new order" in east Asia. Within the sphere of this new order lie French Indo-China and the Netherlands East Indies. The mother countries of those two rich colonies are occupied to-day by German troops. French Indo-China, by the agreement of Hanoi of September 27, opened its gates to Japanese troops in circumstances that strongly suggest German pressure. We may expect further demands on French Indo-China.

The formation of the triple axis has, without doubt, contributed to international tension, particularly in the Far East. It has not, however, served either to intimidate the United States, or to isolate Britain. Indeed, its effect has been the exact opposite. There has been a marked stiffening of policies both of the United States and of Britain in the Far East, and an intensification of sentiment in the United States in support of aid for Britain.

The events of the past few months make it clearer than ever that the immediate aim of Germany is a new world order, based upon spheres of influence to be controlled by Nazi Germany and her axis partners. Hitler plans, by holding out specious hopes of collaboration, to secure the participation of the subject peoples in the elaboration of his grand design. This is the subtle method by which he is supplementing aggression in his effort to achieve world domination.

Nazi intrigue and the deceptive cloak of collaboration fail, however, to conceal the underlying tyranny of force and fear on which the structure of the new order is to rest. It becomes more apparent, with each new development, that we are engaged in a titanic and terrible death struggle between two conflicting philosophies of life. On the one side is tyranny; on the other, democracy. On the one side, brutality and slavery; on the other, humanity and freedom. On the one side, the law of force; on the other, the force of law.

THE NAZI DESIGN

With the collapse of France, practically the whole of Europe, west of Russia, lay prostrate at the feet of Hitler and his Italian ally, who, on the eve of the fall of France, had joined him in the war. The military machine of the Nazis seemed, in June, well nigh invincible. Britain stood alone in the path of the onward march of the conquerors. There she still stands; the one obstacle left in the way of the establishment, in the old world, of the new Nazi order.

What Hitler has failed to accomplish by fear or force—the destruction of Britain—he has now set about attempting to effect by intrigue and guile. A new world order, based upon spheres of influence to be controlled by Nazi Germany and her axis partners, is now the immediate aim. This is the subtle method by which, as the ultimate end of aggression, Germany hopes to attain world domination. Through the alliance between Japan and the axis in Europe the new order in Asia has been linked to the new order in

Europe. The pattern is now plain. The world, as I have said, is to be divided into spheres of influence. Germany and her greater vassals are to dominate a world of lesser vassals. The new order in Asia and the islands of the Pacific is domination by Japan. The new order in Europe is domination by Germany. The new order in the Mediterranean and in Africa is joint domination by Germany and Italy.

The subject peoples will be the menials of the new lords of creation. Their economies will be the economies that satisfy the greed of their masters; their farmers will be peasants, and their workers, slaves. The new Nazi order is not in fact a new order at all. It is a return to despotism and the age-old tyranny against which mankind has ever struggled in its upward march.

CANADA - UNITED STATES JOINT DEFENCE—THE OGDENSBURG AGREEMENT

Recognition of the common interest of the British Empire and the United States in the preservation of freedom, as menaced by the Nazi attempt at world domination, led to agreements of far reaching significance between the governments of the United States and Canada, and the governments of the United States and Great Britain. These agreements may well be found to constitute the most significant development in international affairs during 1940. In importance they far surpass the Triple Axis Agreement concluded by Germany, Italy and Japan.

The session of parliament which adjourned on August 7 was resumed on November 5, 1940. Parliament was thereupon immediately prorogued and a new session begun on November 7. In his speech in the Debate on the Address in reply to the Speech from the Throne, the Prime Minister reviewed developments in the war and the international scene since the August adjournment. In this review he dealt in particular with the joint defence agreements.

CANADA-UNITED STATES JOINT DEFENCE

THE OGDENSBURG AGREEMENT

THE HOUSE OF COMMONS, NOVEMBER 12, 1940

WHEN history comes to record the time and place at which the onward sweep of Nazi aggression was halted, and the tide of war turned, that place and time will be found, I believe, to be the English Channel, during the months of August and September. Just as the evacuation of Dunkirk will remain a chapter unsurpassed in the history of British arms on land, on sea and in the air, so the indomitable resistance of Britain, the stout hearts of the people of London, the unflagging skill and daring of those who fight in the air, and the unceasing vigilance of the navy will mark the supreme moment in the present world conflict, when tyranny was halted in its threatening course, and despair was changed to hope.

There remains little doubt that when French resistance collapsed last June, the government of France and her military leaders believed that not only France but also Britain was doomed. In their despair, they thought that the Nazi onslaught was irresistible and that Britain, too, would crumble before the might of the German attack. The terms of the French surrender and much that has happened since can be understood only in the light of this conviction of Nazi invincibility.

The Myth of Isolaton Dissolved

Nor were the French alone in this appalling belief. It was generally held on the continent of Europe and, to a surprising degree, even in the United States. Public attention there became concentrated on the extent of American preparedness to meet the threat to this hemisphere which would follow the defeat of Britain. The myth of isolation was dissolved in an almost frenzied preoccupation with self-preservation. In order to meet the requirements of United States defences on land and sea and in the air, a movement of opinion developed even to the length of urging the retention in America of supplies of equipment and munitions desperately needed by Britain. Ominous rumours spread and gained credence that Britain could not hold out.

But Britain did hold out, and held out magnificently. The world's vision cleared. Great Britain stood forth as she has through the centuries, an impregnable fortress of freedom. On this side of the ocean despair vanished. The English Channel came to be viewed as the first line of defence of the United States and of the new world. This break in the encircling gloom, this dawn of fresh hope on the horizon, inspired in the United States a new desire to do all that was possible, short of actual war, to aid Britain in her resistance, and in her determination to destroy the enemies of freedom.

The Lines of Defence

The overwhelming majority of the people of the United States came to see in Britain an outwork of their own defence. They saw the need of giving all possible assistance to Britain. But they saw, too, the need for strengthening their second line of defence. If the coasts of America were to be immune from attack, naval and air bases were needed on the islands of the Atlantic. Joint action between the United States and Canada was recognized also as necessary to their common security. From the point of view of Canada and the whole British Commonwealth, what followed constitutes the most significant development in international affairs in the three months since our parliament adjourned in August. In ultimate importance, it far surpasses the formation of the triple axis.

The first inkling of developments already under way was given to the public by the President of the United States, on August 16. On that day Mr. Roosevelt announced that:

> "The United States Government is holding conversations with the government of the British Empire with regard to acquisition of naval and air bases for the defence of the western hemisphere and especially the Panama Canal. The United States Government is carrying on conversations with the Canadian Government on the defence of the western hemisphere."

I shall have something to say to the house in a moment about these conversations. I wish first to recall the events which followed immediately on President Roosevelt's announcement.

The following day, which was August 17, I met the President at Ogdensburg. Our conversations that day, in continuance of conversations previously held, culminated in the formulation of an agreement which was made public the next afternoon, in a joint statement issued by Mr. Roosevelt and myself. I should like now to place the joint statement on record. It has come to be known as the Ogdensburg Agreement. These are its terms:

> "The Prime Minister and the President have discussed the mutual problems of defence in relation to the safety of Canada and the United States.
>
> "It has been agreed that a permanent joint board on defence shall be set up at once by the two countries.
>
> "This permanent joint board on defence shall commence immediate studies relating to sea, land and air problems including personnel and material.
>
> "It will consider in the broad sense the defence of the north half of the western hemisphere.
>
> "The permanent joint board on defence will consist of four or five members from each country, most of them from the services. It will meet shortly."

The Ogdensburg Agreement was reached, as I have said, on August 17, and the joint statement setting forth its terms was issued on the following day. On August 20, Mr. Churchill announced in the British House of Commons the decision of the British Government "spontaneously and without being asked or offered any inducement" to offer the United States sites for naval and air bases in the British possessions in the western hemisphere. I should like particularly to draw the attention of the house to one sentence of Mr. Churchill's announcement of the decision of the British Government. "In all this line of thought," he said, "we found ourselves in very close harmony with the government of Canada."

The Formation of the Permanent Joint Board

On August 22, the Canada-United States permanent joint board on defence was appointed. Colonel O. M. Biggar, K.C., became chairman of the Canadian section and Mayor Fiorello La Guardia of New York, chairman of the United States section. The first meeting of the board was held at Ottawa, in the following week. The board has met since on several occasions, and has been engaged upon continuous study of the sea, land and air problems immediately related to the defence of the north half of this hemisphere.

The next significant announcement came on September 3, the anniversary of the British declaration of war. On that day President Roosevelt announced that an agreement had been reached between the governments of the United Kingdom and the United States by which sites for bases in British Atlantic possessions were to be made available to the United States. In Newfoundland and Bermuda these sites were leased for no other consideration than Great Britain's interest in the strength and security of North America. The other sites in the Bahamas, the British West Indies and British Guiana, forming an outer ring of defence to the Panama Canal, were leased in exchange for fifty over-age United States destroyers.

The house is aware that six of the fifty destroyers have since been made available to the Royal Canadian Navy and are already in commission. During a recent visit to Halifax, I had an opportunity of visiting some of the destroyers about to be transferred and of seeing how completely they were equipped. I was also privileged to extend to the United States admiral who brought the destroyers to Canadian waters the thanks of the government and people of Canada. I had previously written to the President to express our appreciation.

CONVERSATIONS WITH THE PRESIDENT

Now for a word as to the conversations which preceded the Ogdensburg Agreement. The agreement itself was not due to any sudden or precipitate action. It was the outcome of several conversations between the President and myself with respect to coastal defence on both the Atlantic and the Pacific, in which the mutual interests of Canada and the United States were discussed. It has seemed to me that I should reserve for parliament such statement as it might be advisable to make with reference to those conversations which, in their nature, necessarily were highly confidential. I might say I have received the President's permission to refer to them publicly.

In the matter of time and significance, the conversations between President Roosevelt and myself on matters pertaining to the common interest of our two countries in the defence of their coasts, divide themselves naturally into two groups: the conversations which took place prior to the commencement of the war, and those which have taken place since.

The first conversation was on the occasion of a visit I paid the President at the White House, as long ago as March, 1937. At that time the discussion had reference to the position on the Pacific as well as on the Atlantic coasts. It was then agreed that, at some time in the future, meetings might be arranged between the staff officers of both countries to discuss problems of common defence.

On September 30 of that year, the President paid a
visit to Victoria, British Columbia, crossing on a
United States destroyer from Seattle. This visit led
to arrangements for talks between staff officers regarding Pacific coast problems, which took place in
Washington in January, 1938.

I think I may say that on every occasion on which I
have visited the President in the United States, or on
which I have met the President on his visits to Canada,
matters pertaining to the defence of this continent
have been a subject of conversation between us.

The defences on the Atlantic were referred to particularly in our conversations in August, 1938, in the
course of the President's visit to Kingston, and the
opening of the Thousand Islands bridge at Ivy Lea. At
that time, it will be recalled, the President made the
open declaration that the people of the United States
would not stand idly by if domination of Canadian soil
were threatened by any other empire. To this declaration I replied at Woodbridge, Ontario, two days later,
that we too had our obligations as a good, friendly
neighbour.

Our common problems of defence were discussed at
length and in a more concrete and definite way when I
visited Washington in November, 1938, to sign the new
Canadian-United States trade agreement.

In the summer of 1939, the President paid a visit to
Canadian waters off the Atlantic coast. He subse-
quently told me that this visit, like his similar visit to
Victoria two years earlier, had been occasioned by his
concern with the problem of coastal defence.

With the outbreak of war, the question of coast
defences became of vital importance. At the same time,

the fact that Canada was a belligerent and the United
States a neutral complicated the problem of pursuing
the discussions. In the face of the European menace it
was obviously desirable to give expression to the needs
of joint defence. To the means, however, of effecting
this end, the most careful consideration had to be given
in order that there might be no grounds for the belief
that there was any attempt on Canada's part to influence the policies or to interfere in the domestic affairs of a neutral country. Had there not been, between
the President and myself, complete confidence in each
other's purpose and motives, I question if the situation
could have been met without occasioning genuine embarrassment to one side or the other, if not indeed to
both. Fortunately, in the light of our previous conversations, there was no danger of the position being misunderstood, and my visit with the President at Warm
Springs, in April of the present year, afforded an ex-
ceptional opportunity for a careful review of the whole
situation.

This is perhaps an appropriate place for me to say
that, from the beginning, and at the time of each conversation, the President made it perfectly clear that
his primary interest in the subject was the defence of
the United States. I was equally frank in making it
clear that my concern was the effective defence of
Canada, and the defence of the British Commonwealth
of Nations as a whole.

COMMON INTEREST IN DEFENCE OF CONTINENT

If one thing above another became increasingly evi-
dent in the course of our conversations, it was that our
respective countries had a common interest in the mat-

ter of the defence of this continent. Since this was the case, everything pointed to the wisdom of planning carefully in advance for whatever contingency might arise.

The conversations begun between the President and myself before the war, in the direct manner I have described, and at Warm Springs taken up anew after Canada had entered the war, were supplemented as the weeks went by, by conversations conducted through diplomatic channels. Staff conversations followed in due course.

I should perhaps say that I gave to my colleagues who were members of the war committee of the Cabinet my entire confidence with respect to the conversations I had had with the President, and subsequent steps were taken with their knowledge and full approval. I should also like to say that the British Government was kept duly informed of what was taking place. The Canadian Government likewise was kept informed of the defence matters directly discussed between the British Government and the United States. The discussions naturally included questions pertaining to the leasing of air and naval bases on the Atlantic.

As I have already mentioned, the President had announced the day before our meeting at Ogdensburg that conversations had been taking place between the two governments. The Ogdensburg Agreement formally confirmed what the previous conversations and planning had initiated. It made known to the world that plans of joint defence were being studied and worked out between the two countries. It did one thing more: it made clear that the board which was being established to make studies and recommendations was not being formed for a single occasion to meet a particular situation, but was intended to deal with a continuing problem. The board on joint defence was, therefore, declared to be permanent.

By a minute of council approved by His Excellency the Governor-General on August 21, the establishment of the Permanent Joint Board on Defence was formally ratified and confirmed.

RECIPROCITY IN DEFENCE

The Permanent Joint Board on Defence might well be considered a logical development from the declarations made by President Roosevelt and myself in August, 1938. Let me recall these declarations to the minds of hon. members. The vital passage in Mr. Roosevelt's declaration at Kingston on August 18 reads:

"The Dominion of Canada is part of the sisterhood of the British Empire. I give to you assurance that the people of the United States will not stand idly by if domination of Canadian soil is threatened by any other empire."

My acknowledgment of Mr. Roosevelt's Kingston declaration at Woodbridge, Ontario, on August 20, 1938, contained these words:

"We, too, have our obligations as a good friendly neighbour, and one of them is to see that, at our own instance, our country is made as immune from attack or possible invasion as we can reasonably be expected to make it, and that, should the occasion ever arise, enemy forces should not be able to pursue their way, either by land, sea, or air to the United States, across Canadian territory."

These declarations marked the first public recognition by both countries of their reciprocity in defence.

I should be the last to claim that the Ogdensburg Agreement was due wholly to the conversations between the President and myself, or to our reciprocal declarations in 1938. I am happy to know that, in a moment of crisis, personal friendship and mutual confidence, shared over many years between Mr. Roosevelt and myself, made it so easy for us to conclude the agreement reached at Ogdensburg. In reality the agreement marks the full blossoming of a long association in harmony between the people of Canada and the people of the United States, to which, I hope and believe, the President and I have also in some measure contributed. The link forged by the Canada-United States defence agreement is no temporary axis. It was not formed by nations whose common tie is a mutual desire for the destruction of their neighbours. It is part of the enduring foundation of a new world order, based on friendship and good will. In the furtherance of this new world order, Canada, in liaison between the British Commonwealth and the United States, is fulfilling a manifest destiny.

A CENTURY OF FAR-SIGHTED STATESMANSHIP

It cannot be assumed that our common background would, of itself, have produced harmonious relations between the two countries, much as that background has helped to make possible a close understanding between us. The understanding which exists owes its vitality to positive and far-sighted statesmanship over more than a century.

May I recall in this connection the words I used at the opening of the Thousand Islands bridge on August 18, 1938:

"Our populations, after all—"
I said, in referring to Canada and the United States,

"—do not differ from those of Europe. Indeed, the European countries have contributed most to their composition. Each of our countries has its problems of race and creed and class; each has its full measure of political controversy. Nevertheless we seem to have found the better way to secure and maintain our peace.... In the realm of international relations, we, too, have learned to bridge our differences. We have practised the art of building bridges. . . . In the art of international bridge-building there are two structures, each with its association with the St. Lawrence and the great lakes, of which I should like to say just a word. They stand out as monuments of international co-operation and good will. Each has its message for the world of to-day. The one is the Rush-Bagot agreement of 1817; the other, the International Joint Commission created in 1909."

The Rush-Bagot Agreement is a self-denying ordinance of mutual disarmament. The International Joint Commission is an instrument for the peaceful adjustment of differences. The permanent joint board is a mutual arrangement for common defence. All three may appear an inevitable progress dictated by ordinary common sense. But we need only to pause for a moment's reflection to realize that, in the madness of the world to-day, common sense is the highest statesmanship.

Unanimous Approval in Canada and the United States

I doubt if any act by a Canadian Government, and certainly no development in our international relations, has ever received such unanimous acclaim in this country. So far as I have been able to ascertain, not a single newspaper from coast to coast uttered a syllable of disapproval of the Ogdensburg Agreement itself. Though estimates of its importance and of the contribution made by myself may have varied, almost no voice was raised to decry its significance.

Although the presidential campaign was already in progress in the United States, and some effort to make political capital might perhaps have been expected, an examination of American press comment reveals a similar unanimous approval of the Ogdensburg Agreement.

The realization, both in Canada and in the United States, that each nation is obliged to assist in the defence of its neighbour because that is its own best defence, has grown in the two years which elapsed between the Kingston and Woodbridge declarations and the Ogdensburg Agreement.

Contribution to Anglo-American Friendship

The events of those two momentous years have served, as well, to allay the fears of those in Canada who felt that closer relations with the United States would weaken Canada's ties with Britain. Throughout my public life, I have consistently maintained the view that the friendliest relations between Canada and the United States, far from weakening the bonds between the nations of the British Commonwealth, would at all times, prove a source of strength. Moreover, I have always held that in the promotion of Anglo-American friendship, Canada has a very special role to play. This belief, I am happy to say, is shared, in all three countries, by those who have worked for closer relations between the English-speaking communities. It is shared in fullest measure by the present Prime Minister of Great Britain. More than ten years ago, at a time when he himself was holding no public office, Mr. Churchill expressed this belief in terms which I should like to quote from an article of his which appeared in the *Saturday Evening Post* of February 15, 1930.

The words gain a prophetic significance in the light of all subsequent developments and of none more than those of the present day. I quote:

"Great Britain herself has for centuries been the proved and accepted champion of European freedom. She is the centre and head of the British Commonwealth of Nations. She is an equal partner in the English-speaking world.

"It is at this point that the significance of Canada appears. Canada, which is linked to the British Empire, first by the growing importance of her own nationhood, and secondly, by many ancient and sentimental ties precious to young and strong communities, is at the same time intimately associated with the United States.

"The long, unguarded frontier, the habits and intercourse of daily life, the fruitful and profitable connections of business, the sympathies and even the antipathies of honest neighbourliness, make Canada a binder-together of the English-speaking peoples. She is a magnet exercising a double attraction, drawing both Great Britain and the United States towards herself and thus drawing them closer to each other. She is the only surviving bond which stretches from Europe across the Atlantic Ocean. In fact, no state, no country, no band of men can more truly be described as the linch-pin of peace and world progress.''

It is a happy coincidence that the soundness of this view of Canada's position as a link between the British and American peoples should have been so amply demonstrated at a moment when the one who shared it so completely, and who expressed it in such eloquent terms, has come to hold the office of Prime Minister of Great Britain.

VIEWS OF BRITISH PRESS AND STATESMEN

In an editorial comment which appeared in the London *Times* on August 22 of this year, the significance of the Ogdensburg Agreement in the wider relations between the English speaking peoples was recognized in terms reminiscent of Mr. Churchill's utterance of ten years ago:

"The two countries", said the *Times*, "will henceforward have closer ties than they have ever had in the past, and Canada more than ever before will be the linchpin of Anglo-American relations."

Let me quote two other extracts, one from a Labour, and one from a Liberal newspaper. They serve to reveal the unanimity of view of the British press. The London *Daily Herald* said:

"Faith in the British system has been revitalized. So to-day it is with blessing we say: Canada, through you, new links can be forged between us and

our cousins across your unarmed frontier. Make
your own decisions. They are ours.''

On August 20 the *Manchester Guardian* said:

"There is a close connection between the two
announcements of the week-end of the negotiations
with Britain for the leasing by the United States of
naval and air bases in the Caribbean sea and of the
agreement between the United States and Canada
for setting up a joint defence board. They are part
of the preparations for the defence of the western
hemisphere against the dictatorships. They have a
bearing on the war and on American help for
Britain.''

In view of the extent to which, throughout my public
life, my known attitude towards the United States has
been so greatly misrepresented, I may perhaps be pardoned if I venture to give to the house some indication
of how this attitude and my occasional visits to that
country have been viewed by those in the United
Kingdom who are perhaps in the best position to judge
of their value.

In a cable which he sent to me as recently as September 13, and which was first made public in the
United Kingdom, Mr. Churchill was kind enough to
use the following words:

"I am very glad to have this opportunity of thank-
ing you personally for all you have done for the
common cause and especially in promoting a harmony of sentiment throughout the new world. This
deep understanding will be a dominant factor in the
rescue of Europe from a relapse into the dark
ages.''

A few days later—September 17—in the House of
Lords, Lord Caldecote, who was at that time Secretary

of State for the Dominions, made the following reference:

"Perhaps the most striking development in recent weeks has been the coming together of the British Empire and the United States, as illustrated in the recent agreement for the grant of defence bases to the United States in certain British territories and the supply of American destroyers for our naval forces. But this is not all. It has been coupled with and indeed preceded by the agreement between the United States and Canada for the setting up of a joint defence board and perhaps I may be allowed to repeat the tribute which the Prime Minister paid in a recent message to the Canadian Prime Minister, Mr. Mackenzie King, for the great part which he has consistently played in promoting a harmony of sentiment between the British Empire and the United States of America. I need not remind your lordships how pregnant with possibilities this new development may well be for peace and freedom in the years to come."

Any part which our country may have had in bringing about a harmony of sentiment between the British Empire and the United States may well be a legitimate source of pride to all Canadians. In the midst of the darkness which to-day enshrouds mankind, the relations between the United States and the British Commonwealth shine forth as the one great beam of hopeful light left in the world.

A NEW HOPE FOR HUMANITY

During the American Civil War, when the relations between Britain and the United States were strained almost to the breaking point, John Bright, speaking in the British House of Commons on June 16, 1863, used these conciliatory and prophetic words:

"I can only hope that, as time passes, and our people become better informed, they will be more just, and that ill feelings of every kind will pass away; that in future all who love freedom here will hold converse with all who love freedom there, and that the two nations, separated as they are by the ocean, come as they are, notwithstanding, of one stock, may be in future time united in soul, and may work together for the advancement of the liberties and the happiness of mankind."

What greater hope can we entertain for humanity than that the vision of John Bright for the union of souls of the British and American peoples may find its realization in their work together for the preservation of the liberties of mankind.

LIGHTS AND SHADOWS—
THE WAR IN PERSPECTIVE

During the month of November, the heavy bombing of some of the cities of England, the shipping losses on the Atlantic, and the scarcity of the United States exchange required by Britain to pay for much needed war supplies combined to darken the general outlook. In parliament, the seriousness of the situation was reflected in debate. To assist in maintaining a due sense of proportion between reverses and successes in the war as a whole, the Prime Minister sought, in a statement in parliament on December 2nd, so to correlate isolated events that they would appear in their true perspective. In estimating the adequacy of the war effort at any stage, the importance of remembering that, in a long war, Canada's contribution could not be based on the changing circumstances of any particular moment, but that it must be organized to meet future probabilities as well as present needs was also stressed.

For purposes of conference, Hon. J. G. Gardiner, Minister of Agriculture and National War Services, visited London during the months of October and November.

LIGHTS AND SHADOWS—THE WAR IN PERSPECTIVE

THE HOUSE OF COMMONS, DECEMBER 2, 1940

THE HOUSE and the country cannot be reminded too often that the present is not a war of weeks or of months, but of years. This fact must never be lost to sight in viewing the fortunes of war abroad as they vary from place to place and from time to time. Sunshine and shadow are bound to alternate on the wide horizons of a world war. It is inevitable that there will be periods of success and periods of reverse. We would be foolish if we became unduly elated by an immediate triumph; we would be even more foolish if we became depressed by a momentary loss.

It has been the duty of my colleagues and myself, as it would be the duty of any government, to try to see the war steadily, and to see it whole. We have sought never to lose the ultimate in the prospect of the immediate; always to remember that what may appear best to serve the apparent interests of the present may be of ill service to the future. From the very beginning the policy of the present administration has been to plan, in co-operation with the government of the United Kingdom, for a final victorious outcome of the struggle.

Let me give an illustration, the force of which will be immediately recognized. Had we been guided by vociferous demands that were made at the outset, we would have concentrated our effort, our wealth and

181

our strength on recruiting large numbers of men for service in the army overseas, rushing them across the ocean, with conscription as probably the only method of maintaining large supernumerary armies in the field. That might have served to meet a certain clamour of the hour, but, in the long run, it would have made for disunity in Canada, and in meeting Britain's need, have proven to be, in large part, wanton waste. Instead of aiding Great Britain, as we are doing to-day, with our forces in the air and at sea, with munitions, with ships and with other equipment, material and supplies in ever-increasing measure, we would have placed upon a beleaguered island the added burden of feeding numbers of men not required at the present time.

We did not yield to the clamour. The government, instead, laid its plans for a balanced development of all branches. We built up an air force and a navy, as well as an army. We developed war industries, and we conserved exchange for the use of Britain and ourselves. While planning for the battles overseas, we have also been mindful of our own shores, and the dangers with which they may at any moment be beset as the scenes of conflict change and war's terrors become intensified. This type of planning does not lend itself to display. But it brings real results in the end. As it is inevitable that the war will be long, it is equally inevitable that the results of a sustained effort can be realized only with the passage of time.

WAR STRATEGY SOUNDLY PLANNED

While it is true that neither Great Britain nor Canada nor the neutral countries which were invaded foresaw the course of events, it still to-day remains an incontrovertible truth that the broad outlines of British strategy for ultimate victory as planned from the outset are and were fundamentally sound. They contemplated a war, not of months but of years. They envisaged an increase in and the extension of the theatres of military operations. They visualized the necessity, not only of preserving freedom, but the necessity and the obligation to restore it.

From the very beginning, in presenting to this house and to the country the situation as I have had reason to view it, I have tried to speak not from impulse but from reflection. I have hoped that my words might carry the greater weight because they were not too freely and too frequently expressed. I have attempted, in so far as opportunity has permitted, to assess and to weigh the essentials. In almost every statement I have made about the war, I have said the struggle would be long and hard and terrible. I have told the people of Canada how much more serious the war would be than, in its early stages, many people seemed to realize, or have yet fully realized. I said that it would be a war, not of months but of years; that it would not be confined to Europe, but must inevitably spread to other continents; that at the back of all was the intent of world domination. I said, too, at the very outset that the nations of Europe, by placing their faith in neutrality, would find, as a consequence of their blindness and aloofness, that their own national existence might disappear.

In official pronouncements this house and the Canadian people have been told repeatedly that supremacy in the air was necessary for effective defence, and for

the final offence which alone can gain victory. They
have been told with equal emphasis that effective
blockade, through the maintenance of British sea
power, was essential, not only to victory, but to survival. Above all, month in and month out, I have said
with all the force at my command that freedom on this
continent was inseparable from the preservation of
British freedom; also that the preservation of British
freedom was inseparable from the restoration of
human freedom wherever it has been destroyed. I
might add that the corollary is equally true. The restoration of human freedom depends upon the preservation of British freedom until the day comes when
the forces of freedom, under the leadership of Britain,
having mobilized their full strength, march forward
to victory.

SITUATION BETTER NOT WORSE

There can be no doubt in the world that the situation
for Britain and her allies is much better to-day than
it was, not only at the time of the signing of the armistice between France and Germany, but as it developed
in the months which immediately followed the fall of
France. Even Hitler was not prepared for the speedy
capitulation of Norway, Holland, Belgium and France.
While the rapidity of those events shocked us, let it
not be forgotten that it surprised Germany as well.
If Hitler's plans had been in accordance with such a
schedule, it is easily conceivable that German armies
might have landed on Britain's shores. It is possible
that the resistance which could have been offered immediately after the evacuation of Dunkirk would not

have been equal to the awe-inspiring task imposed upon it.

When France signed the armistice she believed, and most of the neutral European countries with her, that all was over with Britain as well as with herself. The great tragedy is that France did not know the truth. Believing that the enemy was invincible, she preferred surrender to the prospect of annihilation. In the United States, majority opinion was swayed for a time by the fear that Britain would be powerless to withstand so formidable a foe. It doubted her power to resist. The American people were asking themselves whether it might not be more prudent to retain the weapons of war, even though they were so desperately needed by Britain, in order that they might defend themselves against a peril which would become irresistible once the peoples of the British Isles were vanquished.

All that has changed, and changed completely. Once again the men and women of the British Isles have revealed their dauntless courage and their ability to fight, and to endure, when their freedom is endangered. Like Cromwell's Ironsides, "they know for what they fight."

When we reflect upon the improved position in the Mediterranean, almost unbelievable three months ago; when we recall the transfer of the American destroyers; the enormous increase in war materials which are flowing from the United States and Canada to the island fortress; when in addition to witnessing the fruits of Canadian planning, we have also the certainty of the continuance of the policy of all possible aid to Britain confirmed by the vote of the American people, how can anyone come to feel, in the light of these facts—which are not the confidential property of the government, but all a matter of public knowledge —that the situation is more serious to-day than it was three or four months ago? It is true that the war is increasing in its fury. But it is also true that in the months that have elapsed since the downfall of France, Britain's strength has steadily increased.

THE BOMBING OF CITIES

It is true that night bombing presents a problem which has not yet been solved. It is true that darkness, while it denies to the marauder the opportunity of discriminate destruction, adds to his opportunity of indiscriminate murder. Against the successes which the enemy may claim for his ruthlessness, there must be offset what it has cost him in men and in planes. The percentage of British losses, both in the British Isles and in Europe, has been many times less. Moreover, Germany, by pursuing the policy of frightfulness, has greatly challenged the spirit of the British people. In the final analysis the war will be won by national character. By his murderous tactics, Hitler has succeeded in showing to the world that a German victory is impossible.

I have said that the area open to British attack is large, and that the flying distances involved are great. By contrast, the area for German attacks is much more limited, and, since the Channel coast affords nearer bases for German aircraft, the flying distance is considerably less. Partly for this reason, very large numbers of German planes have been employed in recent raids, and it is a tribute both to the fighting skill of British pilots and to the increasing destructiveness of ground defences that so small a proportion of German planes have actually succeeded in penetrating outer defences to attack key targets in Britain. German losses in operational planes have been large, but the more serious loss has been in terms of pilots and air crews. It can, of course, be argued that even numerically, superiority in bombing and fighter aircraft will not provide a guarantee against aerial invasion and aerial bombardment. What is certain is that as British aircraft production, aided by a steady flow of pilots from Canada and planes from the United States and Canada, succeeds in narrowing the gap in effective strength between the Royal Air Force and the German air force, the effect of German attacks upon Britain will be diminished, and the scale of British attacks upon enemy and enemy-occupied territory will be correspondingly increased.

The Shipping Losses

Much the same is true of "the loss of shipping as evidenced by press reports," and of the limitation upon financial resources. To view these factors in their true perspective, their extent has to be measured first of all in its relation to the whole, and, secondly, in comparison with losses and shortages which the enemy has experienced and may reasonably be expected further to experience.

The shipping situation is serious, but that does not mean it has suddenly changed the outlook. It is true that, in recent weeks shipping under British ownership and control has been lost at a rate greater than the present capacity of British shipyards to build new

ships. Nevertheless, thousands of ships remain, and
men and supplies are freely carried where allied necessity calls. British shipyards are working at full capacity, and in addition to British shipyards, Canadian,
Australian and American shipyards are building merchantmen and other ships for Britain. The House of
Commons has already been told that in addition to the
naval construction under way in Canada for the British admiralty, eighteen merchant vessels are also to
be built here for the British Government.

Let it not be forgotten that Germany, too, has suffered considerable shipping losses. Almost daily we
hear of another German supply ship sunk off the coast
of Norway, in the North Sea, or in the Channel. German shipping and German barges have been bombed
repeatedly in the channel ports. The great German
shipyards at Hamburg and Bremen, and even in the
Baltic, have been visited again and again by the bombers of the Royal Air Force. In the Mediterranean the
Italian shipping losses have been heavy. On the high
seas, German and Italian merchantmen have disappeared.

The British navy is still supreme on the seas of
battle. Although the British navy in this war, single-
handed, enforces the blockade, and although the coasts
to be blockaded are more extensive, nevertheless the
blockade is proving its effectiveness.

The Financial Burden

The vast quantities of supplies which Britain re-
quires from North America to supplement the de-
ficiencies of her own production must, of course, be
paid for, and, when ordered from the United States,

they must be paid for in American dollars. The problem of providing United States exchange which faces the British Government is a very real one.

The problem of providing United States exchange which faces the British Government is a problem which also faces our own government; for we too must provide for vast outlays of United States dollars to pay for our purchases of essential war material. It may help us to view the financial problem in a true perspective if, as with bombing and with shipping losses, we make comparison with the situation as it is in Germany. While it is true that Britain and Canada are faced with the problem of providing exchange to pay for their purchases in the United States, it is also true that in the United States we have access to the greatest industrial resources in the world.

What is the German situation? Germany, of course, has acquired the industries and resources of France, Belgium, Holland and Czechoslovakia, but outside the borders of Germany and the territories she has conquered she can look to only two important outside sources of supply—Sweden and Russia. The capacity and the willingness of Russia to spare supplies to Germany is very doubtful. In the conquered territories she must keep the workers alive if they are to continue to produce. She must face, too, the ever-present hazard of sabotage.

Nor would Germany's position be materially improved even if she could command the financial resources to which Britain still has access. Germany is in fact unable, except at the cost of fighting and the loss of the men and materials of war, to obtain some of the essentials of war.

Despite these weaknesses, no greater mistake could be made than to minimize the economic gains which have resulted from the German conquests. They can be balanced and exceeded only by the economic and industrial resources of this continent. Whatever difficulties of a financial nature we may be facing, Germany is denied all access, both financial and physical, to the potentially decisive North American sources of supplies.

THE BALKANS AND THE MEDITERRANEAN

Before concluding, I should, perhaps, say one word about the situation in the Balkans and the Mediterranean. As I pointed out at the beginning, we must keep constantly before us the conflict as a whole. The accession under duress of Roumania, Hungary and Slovakia to the axis adds no new strength to the predatory powers. Even if it did, the abstention of Yugoslavia and of Bulgaria has far greater significance.

It will be recalled that in his statement to the House of Commons on November 5, Mr. Churchill mentioned that the balance of forces on the frontiers of Egypt and the Soudan was far less unfavourable than at the time of the French collapse. So far as subsequent information has been made public, it can be said that the British position has been strengthened on all fronts.

The amazing success of the heroic Greek people, reviving as it does the memory of their ancient glories, has not made the European situation more serious than it was. The successes of the Royal Air Force and the British navy in co-operation with the Greek forces have not advanced the cause of Italy and Germany. The state of affairs in Albania, the disorder in Roumania, and the reluctance of Yugoslavia and Bulgaria, have not greatly aided Hitler in the creation of his new order for Europe.

While what I have said may help us to keep a truer perspective as regards immediate happenings and dangers, what I wish most of all to emphasize is that this is only the picture as it presents itself at the moment, and that no one can foretell to what proportions of danger, peril and frightfulness it may develop at any time. We shall completely err if for a moment we fail to recognize how appalling is the danger which threatens, not only Britain, but civilization, and be tempted thereby to relax any and every effort to put forth the utmost of our strength.

Above all else, let us remember how formidable is Germany's present military strength. There has never been anything hitherto comparable to it. Let us remember, too, that her great armies are undefeated; that they are equipped with all the machines of modern warfare; that, excepting Switzerland, all of Europe west of the Vistula, and extending from Sweden to Portugal and Spain, lies under her control. Her own resources of factory and of mine, of men and materials, have been re-inforced by the material power of the nations which she has conquered; to her millions of soldiers and workmen has been added the man-power of the lands she occupies, however reluctant the men of Norway, of Holland, of Belgium, and of France may be to turn their spears against the breast of freedom.

The Greatest Task in History

Upon the forces of Britain has been placed the greatest task in the history of the world. She has to watch and fight, she has to fight in the British Isles and in the seas that surround them, she has to fight in the Mediterranean, in the Middle East, in Africa; she has to watch the Far East, in Hongkong, in Singapore; she has to keep India constantly in mind. Anywhere, at any time, she may find it necessary to send ships and men to meet a new threat to her lines of communication and supply, or to face fresh horrors in some distant quarter of the globe.

This bare recital of facts proves, of course, that the situation is serious, but certainly not more serious than it has been during the last three months. The only difference is that people themselves in all parts of the world are beginning to realize more of the truth. The situation is bound to become increasingly serious as warfare spreads to new seas and shores and as mutual destruction continues, as it most certainly will, with ever-increasing fury. It is wholly probable that we shall witness much of anarchy as well as of war ere the death-grapple between totalitarianism and democracy has told its tale.

No one can say that the world, even now, may not be heading for Armageddon. The one thing that, under the providence of God, may save the world this supreme tragedy is the might of Britain, strengthened, supported and sustained by the power of the British dominions and India, the help of the United States, and such aid as it may yet be within the power of other liberty-loving peoples to give. In order to overthrow the enemy and to save mankind "it is going to take all, that all of us can give."

THE OLD YEAR AND THE NEW

Before the end of the old year, the fortunes of war had greatly favoured the forces of freedom. The British peoples continued to reveal their unconquerable spirit. The invasion of Greece by the Italians, begun on October 28, 1940, had been heroically resisted. Greek forces had carried the war into Albania and successfully occupied a portion of that country. The splendid Greek victories over the Italians were not the only defeats suffered by Italian forces. On the Mediterranean and in North Africa, the British and Imperial forces scored a series of brilliant successes at sea and on land. Mr. Churchill's forecast that the Italian Empire would be torn into shreds and tatters looked as though it were about to be fulfilled.

The Prime Minister seized the opportunity, which the eve of the new year afforded, again to restore a true balance between hopes and fears. Once more he sought to have the conflict viewed as a whole, and to disclose the relationship of events alike to the past, the present and the future. The fate of mankind was said to be in the balance. 1941 was described as likely to be the decisive year.

THE OLD YEAR AND THE NEW

BROADCAST, DECEMBER 31, 1940

A YEAR ago to-night, men and women belonging to nations that still enjoyed their freedom, were comforting their hearts with the thought that the onset of the aggressor would surely be stayed. In a sacredly guarded neutrality, and behind lines of military and economic defence, unbroken, and which they believed to be unbreakable, they felt a security which would protect their countries and their lives. They did not see—indeed, none of us could have believed—that in the year now all but ended, most of the free nations of Europe would be invaded, and, to-day, dominated by Nazi power. Nor did their minds then envisage the treacherous role of Italy. Nor did they contemplate the danger to the existence of democracies in the new world, as well as in the old, in the open alliance of Japan with the axis powers. All these things have happened. They have taught us that the prospect of world domination by a single power and its vassal states is no longer merely the dream of tyranny, or the nightmare of liberty. It is a danger upon the threshold of our very doors.

Fortunately, the old year, which has seen so many misfortunes and horrors, has witnessed other things as well. Foremost has been the unconquerable spirit of the British peoples. It has seen the heroism of Greece, and the mortal thrusts at Italian power in Northern

Africa and the Mediterranean, by Briton and Greek alike. The year that is ending has also witnessed the calling in of the new world to redress the balance of the old. Within recent months, the United States of America has determined to constitute itself, in the words of President Roosevelt, "the arsenal of democracy." The vast storehouses of the industrial sources of the whole North American continent, which, alone, can balance and surpass the industrial strength of Germany, are open to Britain, and closed to her enemies.

To refer more immediately to ourselves, this old year has witnessed a vast increase in our country's capacity to aid in the winning of the war. The Canadian forces have grown in strength on land, at sea, and in the air. Canadian industry, Canadian labour, and Canadian agriculture have worked together to equip and supply our own soldiers, sailors, and airmen; and, in increasing measure, to provide munitions, equipment, supplies, and foodstuffs for Britain. Above all, the year has witnessed, on the part of the Canadian people, a unity of purpose, a determination of effort, and a readiness to make whatever sacrifices may be involved, second only to Britain herself.

It is an exhilarating thing to see the history of brave men repeat itself through the ages. Pride in the heroism of the defenders of Britain and Greece has vastly strengthened the sense of kinship amongst all free peoples. Moreover, realization of the common danger has fortified the common determination of free nations to end, for all time, the menace of tyranny.

THE TREMENDOUS TASK IN THE NEW YEAR

Inspired as we have been by British courage and the brilliant successes of the British and Greek arms in the Mediterranean and Northern Africa, above all else, we must refuse, as we enter upon a new year, to be lulled into the dangerous belief that the tide has definitely turned, and that success is now assured. Such a conclusion would disclose a fatal lack of appreciation of the inherent dangers of the present conflict. The victories in the Mediterranean, however splendid, cannot of themselves decide the issue. Moreover, Italy is not the real enemy. The real enemy is Nazi Germany. Her armies stand to-day unimpaired in their might—as strong, or stronger, than ever. While denied the complete victory they hoped for in 1940, they have, thus far, known only successes. They have never been defeated. While invasion of Britain has been prevented, Nazi warfare in the air and at sea has grown in intensity.

Nor should we count too eagerly upon an early offensive. Instead, we must be prepared for further manifestations of Nazi aggression. The vast resources of conquered Europe are being harnessed by their Nazi masters to drive their war machine. In the valley of the Danube, the Nazi hordes are again possessing themselves of the lands of neighbouring peoples. They are bent on further conquest. The few unconquered nations of Europe live in the shadow of Nazi terror. At the other side of the world, a menacing cloud darkens the Far Eastern sky.

We have everything to gain and nothing to lose by viewing, in all its stark realism, the tremendous task which faces the defenders of freedom. That task may well be greater in 1941 than it has been in 1940. It is going to demand more effort, more sacrifice, and far more change in our daily lives than up to now has been required.

THE FATE OF MANKIND IN THE BALANCE

I wish I could believe that the New Year will see the end of the present conflict. That, of course, is a possibility. While the signs of the times are the stars of hope, and not the black omens of despair, they point, nevertheless, to an expansion rather than to a contraction of the areas of conflict, and of the theatres of war. I do believe, however, that the year 1941 will see a decisive tilting of the balance in which ultimate victory and defeat are being weighed; and that, ere its close, we shall be able to read something of the future which will be our own. That future, I doubt not, will be a new world order which will cherish freedom, truth, and justice. It will be born of all there has been of toil and of prayer, of suffering and of sacrifice.

The heroic endurance by the men, women, and children of Britain in the midst of fire and death from the clouds; the determination of ordinary men and women to carry on with their work amid the wrecks of their homes and in peril of their lives; the gallant resistance of the whole of Britain in the face of terrible odds; these things have taught us that the Nazi might is not invincible. They have taught us, too, that none is too humble to do his part in upholding the cause of freedom.

Some of our tasks may seem to be remote from the

making of war. But every duty well and honestly done is a contribution to victory. Let each one of us, whether he works in the factory or on the farm, in the forest or in the mine, at the desk or in the home, labour at his appointed task with all the strength of his arm, and a prayer in his heart. Liberty in the Old World—everywhere in the world—will depend upon labour in the New World.

1941: THE DECISIVE YEAR

To-night, I appeal to you, my fellow-Canadians, with all the earnestness of which I am capable, to enter upon the New Year resolved to maintain above everything that unity of purpose, of determination, and of effort, in the winning of the war, which has been, from the outset, and will remain till the end, the secret of our strength. Let us consecrate our individual lives and the collective life of Canada to the preservation of freedom. Let us work and pray for its restoration in all lands which have lost their liberty. It is my firm belief that the events of the New Year will determine for our generation, and for many generations to come, the fate of mankind. The present struggle can have but one of two outcomes. Either tyranny, based on brutality, must be overthrown, or the free peoples of the world, one and all, slowly but inevitably be reduced to a state of bondage.

Let us remember that when we speak of the preservation of democracy, of Christianity, and of civilization, we use no idle words. They are inseparably intertwined, one with another. It is the existence of all three that is at stake. The events of the year 1941 will determine whether this precious heritage will survive.

A RESOLVE FOR THE NEW YEAR

As I conclude this broadcast, at the close of the old year, my thoughts are with the colleagues who have shared with me the responsibilities of government since the commencement of the war. I recall the singleness of purpose and high devotion with which they have given of their time and strength to their appointed tasks. Particularly have I in my memory the one of our number who was taken so suddenly from our midst.

Canada will not soon forget the services given to her by the late Norman McLeod Rogers. As Minister of National Defence at the time, he had just returned from a visit to Britain where he had conferred with the British authorities upon the best way in which Canada could help with the conduct of the war. On the desk, in Mr. Rogers' office, after his death, were found, in his own handwriting, words in which he recorded his faith and his hope. His faith remains to inspire us; his prophecy is still our hope. For the New Year, as individuals and as a nation, we can form no higher resolve than to make his words our own. They belong to the old year, but they belong even more to the new. It will be found, I believe, that they belong perhaps not to any year, but to all time.

Here are Mr. Rogers' words:

"In the faith we will fight on, we will resist, we will endure, we will take the offensive, and we will win."

TOTAL WAR AND TOTAL EFFORT

Parliament adjourned on December 7, 1940, and reassembled on February 17, 1941. During the parliamentary recess Hon. J. L. Ralston, Minister of National Defence, and Hon. C. D. Howe, Minister of Munitions and Supply, visited Britain and personally conferred with the United Kingdom authorities. The purpose of the visit was to emphasize, and to translate into the most effective action, the determination of the Canadian people to put forth their utmost strength in the cause of freedom. It was also to gain, at first hand, further information as to how Canada's resources might best be used to achieve a maximum effort. On the basis of the reports made by the Ministers upon their return, the War Committee of the Cabinet completed its decision on Canada's war programme for the new year. The programme was announced by the Prime Minister in a nation-wide broadcast on February 2nd. The broadcast was also made the occasion for a war savings appeal.

TOTAL WAR AND TOTAL EFFORT

BROADCAST, FEBRUARY 2, 1941

THERE are many indications that, within a very short while, the enemy will make a tremendous effort to destroy the British Commonwealth by a series of smashing blows of unprecedented severity. Total war will be waged in all its fury. Hitler has made his purpose clear. It will be a desperate race against the growing power and strength of the British Commonwealth, a strength augmented by steadily increasing supplies from the United States.

TOTAL WAR AND HOW TO MEET IT

We have heard a great deal about total war. Total war means an indiscriminate attack on every front, by every means, however fiendish. It is war on sea, on land, and in the air, against armed forces and forts, warships and merchant ships. Practised by the Nazis, as we have seen, it is war against homes, hospitals, schools and churches. It is war on men, women and children. It is war by shot, shell, fire and poison gas. Its aim and purpose are total destruction. This is the war with which Britain is face to face. We would soon know all its horrors if the enemy could reach us. Between this continent and that attack, Britain stands as the first line of defence.

There is only one way to meet total war, and that is by total effort—effort not for a day, or a week, or a month, but every day until victory is won.

Total effort means that every man, woman and child does and keeps on doing everything possible to help.

Total effort can be achieved in two ways. It can be compelled by dictatorial force—that is the enemy's way. It can be obtained by the free-will offering of a free people—that is our way, and the way we must strive to preserve. We are a free people, and every day since the war began, there has been proof of the growing willingness of our people to spare no effort or sacrifice, that the needs of the war demand.

A TIME FOR SACRIFICE

When I spoke to you on New Year's Eve, I told you that the year 1941 would require more effort, more sacrifice, and far more change in our daily lives than we had known or made in 1940. No task, I said, is too humble, no labour too insignificant, no individual too poor or too weak to make a contribution to the winning of the war.

Our contributions are being made in many ways. Tens of thousands of our young men are in the army, the navy, and the air force. Hundreds of thousands of men and women are working in factories, on farms, in mines and forests and by the sea. Many more thousands are deeply stirred with a passionate desire to help. Not everyone can fight in the front line, or make war supplies. But almost everyone can help to provide the money which is necessary to feed, equip and transport the fighting forces, and to make the weapons and munitions of war. Now that the skies are full of sure signs of a gathering storm, the government of your country appeals to you to lend what assistance you can, as quickly as you can.

THE PROGRAMME FOR 1941—NAVY, ARMY, AIR

On the programme for 1941 which has been worked out by the War Committee of the Cabinet, there is, I am pleased to say, complete agreement between the British and Canadian Governments. This programme involves a number of new measures. It represents a co-ordinated effort based upon Canada's utmost productive capacity.

The new measures are being so timed as to fit into the programme of the Admiralty, the War Office, the Air Ministry, and the Supply departments of the United Kingdom.

The expansion of the Royal Canadian Navy will continue at a rapid rate. The navy had a strength, at the beginning of the war, of 15 ships and 1,774 men on active service. To-day ,the strength of the navy is 175 ships and 15,319 men of all ranks. The present plan will bring the navy up to an estimated strength by March 31, 1942, of 413 ships and 26,920 men.

Canadian ships are at present serving in the Atlantic and the Pacific, both North and South, in the Caribbean, and in European waters. Canadian sailors, in the Canadian navy, or attached to the Royal navy, are on duty on all of the Seven Seas.

The plan for our active army for 1941 includes the despatch overseas, successively, of the following formations:

(1) the balance of the Corps Troops for the Canadian Corps of two divisions now in England;

(2) an Army Tank Brigade for employment with the Canadian Corps. This will enable Canada to be repre-

sented in the United Kingdom by a Canadian armoured formation which will be attached to and operate with the Canadian Corps, thus providing increased striking power;

(3) the Third Canadian Division, with its complement of Corps Troops;

(4) a Canadian Armoured Division.

All these army projects have been approved by our National Defence staff, by Lieutenant-General McNaughton, and by the staff of the British War Office. There is complete agreement on the timing and extent of the measures which it is proposed to take.

Throughout 1941 we shall continue the vigorous and energetic development of the Air Training Plan. All the projects and schools connected with the Plan will be opened, and in operation, before September of this year. This represents a clear gain of eight months on the original schedule. The aerodrome construction this year will be equal in extent to that of last year. Through the recruiting of airmen and air crews, the present strength of 36,000 men will be doubled. The present number of 1,700 aeroplanes now in use in the Training Plan will be increased to well over 4,000 before the end of the year.

In Canada, our air defence will be strengthened by an increase in the number of operational squadrons attached to the Home War Establishment.

Overseas, the three Canadian squadrons, fully equipped, manned and maintained by Canada, will be kept up to strength. There will, in addition, be constituted out of the graduate pupils of the Joint Air Training Plan, and identified as Canadian, twenty-five new squadrons. Under the terms of the Air Training Plan Agreement, as you may recall, these squadrons are to be equipped and maintained by the United Kingdom. In addition to the men who will form these squadrons, many thousands more young Canadians, who are graduates of the Plan, will go forward to Britain to take their place in the battle line of the air, alongside their comrades from Australia, New Zealand, and the United Kingdom.

WAR PRODUCTION AND SUPPLIES

A vast increase in production in war equipment and supplies has been arranged. As the United States is prepared to manufacture for Britain only such munitions as are in common use for United States' war purposes, Canadian armament production during 1941 will be concentrated on types of war equipment and weapons which are not obtainable in the United States, such as: tanks, small arms, machine-guns, anti-aircraft and anti-tank guns. The production of a wide range of naval guns and field guns will be enlarged; Canada is the only source of supply outside Britain for these guns. Canada will also specialize on the production of ammunition for these weapons, and on the manufacture of explosives.

Canada is now the only source of supply outside Britain for motor transport vehicles. You will, I am sure, be pleased to know that practically all of the motor vehicles in use in the African campaign have been and still are of Canadian manufacture. Canadian workmen may well take pride in their share in the victories of Libya.

Canada's shipbuilding industry has already constructed many small naval vessels. A number of these are operating in European waters. We are also building merchant ships in increasing numbers. We propose to undertake the building of destroyers in Canadian shipyards.

Our aircraft industry will concentrate on building in Canada enough aeroplanes for the Air Training Plan. At Britain's request, our surplus capacity will be used for the manufacture of long-range bombers which can be flown across the Atlantic.

It will be apparent that the needs of the armed forces and of war industry will make large demands upon available Canadian man-power. It is estimated that, for the purposes mentioned, 200,000 additional men and women will be required during the present year. Of this number at least 75,000 must be skilled or semi-skilled workers. The federal government, in co-operation with the provincial governments, is establishing vocational and plant training schools capable of training 100,000 persons a year.

To do all these new things, and to continue the work already in hand, will tax Canada's productive capacity to the limit. It will necessitate more of a shift from peace-time to war-time production, and a cutting down of luxury production, and of luxury buying. It will mean more in the way of united determination, effort and sacrifice than has ever before been asked of the Canadian people. We have also to keep in mind the financial assistance which Canada is undertaking in financing purchases of the United Kingdom in this country.

War Effort Dependent on Individual Effort

Every saving you lend to Canada will help to make possible the attainment of the war effort I have outlined. Your savings, standing alone, may seem small and insignificant. But taken together, the savings of all the citizens of Canada, may well weight the scales on the side of victory.

In the midst of the dark days of the last war, the then Prime Minister of Great Britain, in appealing to his countrymen, related to them an old Celtic legend. It seems to me in his appeal, and in the simple tale which it relates, there lies a lesson for us all.

"There is a story", said he, "of a man who was given a series of what appeared to be impossible tasks to perform, ere he could reach the desires of his heart. Amongst other things he had to do, was to recover every grain of seed, that had been sown in a large field, and bring it all in, without one missing, by sunset. He came to an ant-hill, and won all hearts and enlisted the sympathies of the industrious little people. They spread over the field, and, before sundown, the seed was all in except one grain; and, as the sun was setting over the western skies, a lame ant hobbled along with that grain also. Some of us have youth, and vigour, and suppleness of limb; some of us are crippled with years or infirmities, and we are, at best, but lame ants. But we can all limp along with some share of our country's burden, and thus help her in this terrible hour, to win the desire of her heart."

Freedom's Crowning Hour

As, in Canada, we each seek to serve as best we can, let us not be misled into believing that because we have not been assigned some special role, our contribution

in effort or in saving may be too slight to be of value
to so great a cause. It is for each one to seek out for
himself, in the circumstances in which he finds himself, how he can best play his part. Example sufficiently
inspiring will surely be found in the lives of the men
and women of Britain. Neither let us be dismayed at
the magnitude of the task, nor discouraged by the
length of the road. Across the centuries, there come to
us, as there came to the defenders of the faith in
ancient days, words which have sustained the human
heart in all its struggles:

> "Let us not be weary in well-doing; for in due
> season we shall reap, if we faint not".

> "Ye, that have faith to look with fearless eyes
>   Beyond the tragedy of a world at strife,
> And know that out of death and night shall rise
>   The dawn of ampler life,
> Rejoice, whatever anguish rend your heart,
>   That God has given you the priceless dower
> To live in these great times and bear your part
>   In Freedom's crowning hour;
> That ye may tell your sons who see the light
>   High in the heavens—their heritage to take;
> I saw the powers of darkness put to flight,
>   I saw the morning break."

BRIGHTER SKIES AND GATHERING
STORMS—THE WAR IN REVIEW

When parliament reassembled on February 17, 1941, the interval of adjournment had witnessed a considerable change in the European scene. The Italian forces had experienced a series of humiliating defeats. British prestige had greatly increased on the continent of Europe and in America. The attitude of the United States had become definitely one of lending all possible assistance to Britain and to other nations resisting aggression. So much brighter did the skies appear that there was real danger of an under-estimation of Hitler's strength and of erroneous comparisons being drawn between the present and the last war.

On the opening day of the session, the Prime Minister once again sought to picture the international situation in its true light, to take account not less of gathering storms than of brighter skies. The review was intended also to afford a background against which the Minister of Finance, on the day following, was to introduce a war appropriation bill for the unprecedented sum of $1,300,000,000. At the time of the introduction of this measure, the Minister stated that, including the financial aid afforded to Britain, the Canadian people would be required to place in all, at the disposal of the government, about half the national income.

BRIGHTER SKIES AND GATHERING STORMS —THE WAR IN REVIEW

THE HOUSE OF COMMONS, FEBRUARY 17, 1941

EARLY in December I gave reasons for the view that the situation for Britain and her allies was much better than it had been, not only at the time of the collapse of France, but in the months that followed that appalling catastrophe. The development of events has borne out the justness of that view. In the United Kingdom, night bombing raids, which were then the subject of so much anxiety, have become not more, but less effective. Submarine attacks, though continuing to constitute the gravest menace, have, in fact, in recent weeks, grown not more, but less destructive. In spite of enemy attempts at interference, the output of British industry has developed at a faster tempo and on a wider scale. On land, on sea and in the air the defences of the British Isles have been materially strengthened. The morale of the British people has remained unshaken. If anything, the entire population has become more determined than ever. In Europe the Royal Air Force has effected large scale destruction of industrial plants and agencies of communication, and of naval and air bases, particularly the so-called invasion ports. The British navy has continued to patrol waters adjacent to the British shores, and to protect the transportation of men, munitions and supplies to and from the British Isles and other parts of the Empire.

Italian Fascist Regime Discredited

In the African campaign, the whole situation has changed, from one of grave uncertainty for the British, to one of the gravest concern for Italy. Spectacular victories have been gained over the enemy in the field. The whole Italian Empire in Africa is vanishing before the eyes of the world.

Across the Mediterranean, in Albania, the Italians have fared no better. The Greek army, fighting with a valour worthy of the finest traditions of classical times, has inflicted on the Italians a whole series of defeats. Thus far re-inforcements from across the Adriatic have wholly failed to reverse the tide of battle.

Success in arms is a potent factor in international affairs. That Britain, half armed and preoccupied with the defence of the British Isles, was strong enough and courageous enough to spare men and materials of war for service in Africa; that the British fleet has been able to patrol the narrow waters of the Mediterranean and even in broad daylight to bombard Genoa, the leading Italian seaport; that assisted by the British naval and air force a small Greek army has repeatedly defeated vastly better equipped and more numerous Italian forces; these facts have undoubtedly served greatly to strengthen British prestige. They have helped to maintain the confidence of Turkey, Egypt, and the Arab world. They have served to encourage the resistance of France and Spain to the pressure of German demands.

To view these facts in their true perspective, however, we must also recognize what Nazi penetration has meant to Roumania and what the dread of a like fate means to-day to Bulgaria and Yugoslavia. We should also keep in mind that the victories have been won against the minor and not the major axis partner. Italian power is one thing; the might of Nazi Germany is quite another.

The Italian defeats to which I have alluded have a further significance. They have shown in unmistakable fashion that, while the Italian soldier has been led into war, his heart is not in the cause. It would be difficult otherwise to explain the apathy, discontent and indifference which have marked the conduct of operations on the Italian side. Numbers are important and equipment is important, but neither one nor both of them can make up for a lack of fighting spirit. The Fascist regime has been discredited in the eyes of its own people. The Italian people are not, and in this war have never been, behind Mussolini. As Mr. Churchill said in his broadcast to the people of Italy on December 23, the Italians have been forced into alliance with the Nazi aggressors by one man, against the will of the king and the royal family of Italy, against the Pope and all the authority of the Vatican and of the Roman Catholic church, and against their own wishes. Could anything illustrate more completely the power and the dangers of dictatorship?

UNITED STATES ASSISTANCE TO DEMOCRACIES

I now turn to a development of very great significance. It is the change which has taken place in the attitude of the United States. It serves by contrast to illustrate the methods of a democracy in safeguarding its interests and asserting its power. The rapid crystallization of opinion in the United States in favour of actively assisting the democratic countries in their struggle against aggression has been the most important event of the present year and the months immediately preceding.

The earlier policy of the United States was devised before the war started. It was based upon an assumption which ignored the real character of the present struggle. American ships were withdrawn from British waters and forbidden to enter the war zone; the belligerents were allowed to buy only what they could pay for and themselves carry away. Purchases were limited to such as could be made in the course of normal business. The unanswerable logic of events has brought home to the American people the realization that their future development, their security, the survival of the democratic way of life, are all bound up inseparably with the defence of Britain and the defeat of aggression. The President's message to Congress, one of the most important in his great career, set forth in words which cannot be misunderstood, a new policy of full material support of peoples resolute in resisting aggression. It expressed the determination of the United States that the cause of freedom shall prevail.

The President's message is more than a statement of principles. It deals with means as well as with ends. The new policy as laid down by Mr. Roosevelt envisages sending ships, planes, tanks and guns to beleaguered Britain and to other nations resisting aggression. This aid is to be furnished in ever-increasing measure without the exaction of immediate payment and regardless of the threats of dictators. To the whole democratic world the new policy has brought fresh hope and renewed resolution.

The United States is without question the most powerful economic unit in the world. The forces against which the mobilization of this vast, this unrivalled industrial power is directed, must eventually feel the full weight of the impact. Meanwhile its growing might gathers like an impending avalanche above the heads of the aggressor nations.

That the material assistance of the United States on the scale contemplated will in the long run be of decisive importance, there can be no shadow of doubt. We must make sure, however, that there is a long run. A very critical stage is certain to be reached before the full aid of the United States becomes available. The skies are full of sure signs of a gathering storm.

REALISTIC VIEW OF SITUATION

Where the storm will break we cannot say. It may come in the Near East, or in the western Mediterranean, or in the Far East, or over Britain itself. It may come in more than one place at the same time. Signs are not lacking that it may come in all these places at once. Among diplomatic and military authorities there is a growing belief in the possibility of a world-wide conflagration involving an attempted German invasion of Britain timed with thrusts at Suez and Gibraltar and a Japanese thrust at Singapore. The German air force and army may try to break Britain; simultaneously the combined axis powers may try to seize Britain's most strategic positions, Gibraltar, Suez and Singapore.

It would be the gravest of errors to assume that growing alarm and tension in the Balkans mean that Hitler is abandoning his attack upon the British Isles. It is British power that Hitler is out to destroy, and the seat of it is the island fortress in the North Sea. It is no less apparent that the destruction of British power is the bond that cements the axis powers. Only by the defeat of Britain can the combined totalitarian powers gain their world sway. It is well that this fact should be constantly and squarely faced. There is, moreover, nothing to be gained by failing to view the strategic world picture in its true proportions. On the contrary there is everything to be gained by seeing it as a whole and in its true light. It is to the emergence of this wider vision that Britain and her allies owe the ever-increasing aid from the United States.

If I venture again to draw attention to the situation as it must present itself in any realistic view, it is not because I wish to lessen the optimism to which the successes thus far achieved have naturally given rise, but rather to see that they do not blind us to the real struggle which has still to be faced, and which I believe is even now at hand. That the forces of freedom will triumph in the end, I have no doubt whatever. But equally I believe, as I have already so frequently said, that the road is going to be much harder, much longer and much more terrible than most people imagine. We should govern our thoughts and actions accordingly.

The enemy must be held back until his strength can be matched. That day will not come soon. Long, grim months lie ahead, in which we must expect set-backs and discouragements. In the present circumstances it is more than ever necessary to steel our hearts and minds to the magnitude of the effort, and of the sacrifice, that will be demanded of us over a considerable period of time and, in a special measure, throughout the next few months. We are too prone to think of the outcome of the last great war and to draw our conclusions from it. It is well, therefore, that we should check up comparisons with the last war at all possible points.

COMPARISONS WITH LAST WAR

First, then, let us remember that the resources and striking power of the enemy are vastly greater than they were in the first Great War.

The forces arrayed against us are not only vastly greater, they occupy a strategic position far more favourable than they did at that time. Then, by heroic efforts in which our Canadian divisions played an important part, the allied and associated powers were able to hold the line, and save the Channel ports. To-day the whole coast from Norway to Spain, from the Arctic Ocean to the Bay of Biscay, is in enemy hands. The enemy is enabled to send his raiders far out into the Atlantic. Moreover, to help in combating them we no longer have the powerful French navy at our side. Instead, we are hourly reminded that the enemy is seeking an excuse to seize the French fleet and French Mediterranean ports, to be used as weapons and bases against us.

In the air as well as at sea the strategic character of the war has also changed to the enemy's advantage. The development of aviation has vastly reduced the insular security of Britain. Hers is no longer an unmolested workshop. Factories, arsenals and shipyards have their schedules upset and their output reduced by bombardment from the air, and even more by the loss of time arising from the stopping of work during air raids. Moreover, Britain's vulnerability to air attack is relatively greater than the enemy's, due to the concentration of Britain's population and her industry, and to her dependence on overseas supplies of food, materials and munitions.

These basic difficulties in the situation should constantly be kept in mind. The very assurance of moral support, of moral and material help from the United States, is not without its bearing upon the immediate problem. With the long term issue automatically decided against the enemy if he remains inactive, Germany must now stake everything on a supreme effort to destroy the British Commonwealth before the resources of the United States are fully mobilized. We may be perfectly sure that this is Hitler's plan of campaign. No man can tell how fast or how far the red fires of war will spread before the conflagration can be brought under control. The determining factor in the matter of time is likely to be the situation as it develops in the ensuing weeks in Europe itself.

FRANCE, JAPAN, THE UNITED STATES

Few if any events have affected Canadians more profoundly than the tragic fate that has befallen France. We have not permitted her misfortunes to lessen our efforts on her behalf. Convinced that we are fighting her battle as well as our own, we are continuing our diplomatic relations with her, in the firm belief that whatever the pressure put upon her by an unscrupulous enemy, France will suffer herself to be destroyed before she will take up arms against Britain, or permit her fleet or naval bases on the Mediterranean to fall into German hands.

The diplomatic position with respect to France is, of course, delicate, because of the fact that the French Government, overwhelmed by the German onslaught, has entered into an armistice with the enemy. We in Canada, however, have no wish to add to the heavy burdens and difficulties which she is facing under the heel of a ruthless and arrogant conqueror, and so long as France takes no action that is contrary to the interest of Canada or her allies, there are the strongest of reasons why we should continue our present relations. We are well aware of the pressure which the enemy is exerting to secure her collaboration in the organization of Europe under German hegemony and control. We will, however, do nothing to stir up bitterness or recrimination over what is past, but will ever seek to encourage the French people to remain true to their great tradition, and to find once again their historic position in Europe and their high place in the comity of nations.

The situation in the Far East has unfortunately continued to give cause for growing apprehension—an apprehension which is not lessened by the recent Japanese intervention as a mediator in the dispute between French Indo-China and Thailand, the new name for the old kingdom of Siam. The decision of the Japanese Government to ally itself with Germany and Italy, under certain conditions, has undoubtedly greatly increased tension in the whole Pacific area. We have done what we could do to lessen that tension and to avoid any occasion for its further development. In a period when national passions are aroused, a period which is marked by so much suspicion of motives and of aims, when it is so easy to engender misunderstanding and ill will, we have tried to avoid any occasion for provocation or offence, we have sought to avoid propagandist activity, we have followed developments with forbearance and restraint, and have done our utmost to conserve a maximum of good will in a strife-torn world.

In a world in which the old methods of free and open discussion, and the old objectives of close and friendly collaboration between nations, have been so greatly curtailed, and over so large an area have disappeared altogether, it is a matter of special satisfaction that, in spite of the stresses and strains of war, our relations with our great neighbour, the United States, have, if anything, grown more cordial, friendly, helpful, and constructive. It is particularly gratifying also to see that there exists not only between our two governments but between our two nations, so perfect an understanding. Our own relations with the United States form but a part, a segment, of the great circle of friendships which now draw together the peoples of the English-speaking world.

A MILESTONE OF FREEDOM—
THE LEND-LEASE ACT

The new year had scarcely begun before President Roosevelt, on January 6, 1941, delivered to the Congress of the United States the great message in which he set forth the policy which shortly afterwards was incorporated in the Lend-Lease Bill. The new policy envisaged sending ships, planes, tanks, guns and other war supplies to beleaguered Britain, and to other nations resisting aggression. This aid was to be furnished in ever-increasing measure without the exaction of immediate payment and regardless of the threat of dictators. To the whole democratic world the announcement brought fresh hope and renewed resolution. In Congress the bill was debated at length. It was passed on March 11 and, on the same day, was signed by the President.

A MILESTONE OF FREEDOM — THE LEND-LEASE ACT

THE HOUSE OF COMMONS, MARCH 12, 1941

THE signature by the President of the United States of the Lend-Lease Bill, after its passage by large majorities in the House of Representatives and the Senate, will stand throughout time as one of the milestones of freedom. It points the way to ultimate and certain victory. The majorities given to the measure in Congress are evidence that this law carries with it the overwhelming approval of the citizens of the United States. It is a declaration by the President, in the name of its government and people, that the United States is determined to supply such aid in the present war as will ensure but one end to the conflict. That end will be its successful termination by the defeat of the aggressor nations, and the preservation, restoration and expansion of freedom wherever the aggressors have substituted might for right, and national force for international justice.

On February 17, I referred to the change which had taken place in the attitude of the United States. At that time the change had already been reflected in the President's message to Congress.

"The President's message," I said, "is more than a statement of principles. It deals with means as well as with ends. The new policy as laid down by Mr. Roosevelt envisages sending ships, planes, tanks

225

and guns to beleaguered Britain, and to other nations resisting aggression. This aid is to be furnished in ever-increasing measure without the exaction of immediate payment and regardless of the threats of dictators. To the whole democratic world the new policy has brought fresh hope and renewed resolution.''

On June 7 of last year, at a time when the news from France was growing daily more ominous, and the entry of Italy into the war was expected at any moment, I said, in a broadcast to the Canadian people:

"If new enemies oppose us, we may be sure that old and new friends will arise to help us. The worldwide significance of the conflict is being realized in every land."

That prediction has been abundantly fulfilled. The friendship of the United States, strengthened by old ties of sympathy, and new ties of practical understanding, has been organized and mobilized upon the side of freedom. This happy consummation has been achieved not by propaganda but by deeds—the brave deeds of the people of Britain, and the wanton and cruel deeds of the tyrants of Germany and Italy. As ruthless act has followed ruthless act, the issues of the conflict have become clear for all to see. The progress of hostilities has been marked by the growing apprehension of the United States. That great country now knows what Nazi and Fascist threats mean in terms of its own freedom, and the happiness of its own citizens. The growing apprehension and increased knowledge have been marked by the cumulative determination of the American people to spare no material effort necessary to help the triumph of the cause which has already commanded the support of their sentiments and their ideals.

THE VOICE OF AROUSED AMERICA

What the passage of this bill means to Britain, and to the cause for which we fight, may well be the difference between prolonged and indecisive warfare, and the certainty of victory. The people of Canada have never doubted what the great-hearted people of the United States would do. Of their own free will, and by their own decision, the American people have spoken in words which tyrants and free men alike will understand. It is as though by one short enactment the world's conscience has condemned the wanton aggressors who have placed freedom, Christianity and civilization in jeopardy.

As the chairman of the Foreign Relations Committee said yesterday in the House of Representatives, the Lend-Lease Bill, "is the voice of aroused America, sounding the trumpet call of victory for free government everywhere."

The courage, determination and fortitude of the people of Britain in the face of continuous and appalling danger have not only gained the ungrudging admiration of the American people, but they have proved, with inexorable logic, that the strength of Britain is the one great obstacle in the path of the aggressors. The American people know that the magnificent resistance of Britain has made her the main outwork of the defences of the United States. Canada's example, as a nation of the new world, actively participating to the utmost limit in the present struggle, has also had its influence in arousing the people of the United States to their present realization that freedom itself is at stake in this war.

It in no sense minimizes the magnificent effort of Britain and the nations of the British Commonwealth to say that the aid, the co-operation and the limitless resources of the United States definitely ensure final victory.

We in Canada may feel more than a little pride in the share we have had in bringing about the closer relationship between the United States and the British Commonwealth. It will, I believe, seal the spiritual union of free peoples everywhere. Out of such a union we may well hope to build an enduring new world order.

A NEW WORLD ORDER

In the month of March, six voluntary organizations, the Canadian Legion, the Knights of Columbus, the Salvation Army, the Young Men's Christian Association, the Young Women's Christian Association and the Imperial Order of the Daughters of the Empire joined in a nation-wide co-operative campaign for aid in providing those auxiliary services so necessary to preserve the moral, and to sustain the physical and spiritual well-being of the fighting forces.

On the joint invitation of the officers of the Canadian War Services Fund and the Canadian Government, Mr. Wendell Willkie visited Canada to lend his voice to the appeal of the War Services organizations. The campaign was opened at Toronto, on the 24th of the month. The Prime Minister, who extended Canada's welcome to Mr. Willkie, expressed the conviction, in the course of his remarks, that the way to an enduring new world order would be found in the application, in all human relationships, of the principle of service exemplified by the work of the War Services organizations. The new order, he believed, would emerge from the one great brotherhood of the English-speaking peoples which their common defence of freedom had already begun to create.

A NEW WORLD ORDER

BROADCAST, TORONTO, MARCH 24, 1941

I HAVE said that the Lease-Lend Act will stand throughout time as a milestone of freedom: that it points the way to ultimate victory. While that is true, it is not less true that Britain continues to stand to-day, as she has through centuries of the past, the cornerstone of freedom in the world.

A UNION OF EFFORT

To-day, all War Service organizations place their experience and their wisdom at the service of our country's war-time needs. Their union of effort means that every contribution will be collected more efficiently, and spent more economically. Practically every dollar which they receive will be dedicated to the shelter, the comfort, the education and the help in other ways of the men and women of our country on guard at freedom's gates in Britain, in Canada, on the islands of the Atlantic and wheresoever the call to service takes them.

Where duty leads our soldiers, sailors, and airmen, these, their friends and helpers, will follow. They will keep alive for those who are far away, the memory of loved ones and the sacred associations of home. In many a hut, and meeting place, and hall of entertainment, the men of our armed forces, under the strain of war, will be afforded moments of rest and relaxa-

231

tion. Amid pleasant and wholesome surroundings, they will be able to sing the songs that cheer them, to write their letters, and to meet those who will be helpful to them. They will, too, be taught many useful things, and will be kept close to the faith and influence of the homes that have moulded and sanctified their lives.

A New World Order

Much is being said to-day about a new world order to take the place of the old world order when the war is at an end. If that new order is not already on its way before the war is over, we may look for it in vain. A new world order cannot be worked out, at some given moment, and reduced to writing at a conference table. It is not a matter of parchments and of seals. That was a part of the mistaken belief at the end of the last war. It is born, not made. It is something that lives and breathes; something much closer to the soul of man; something that needs to be worked out and prepared in the minds and the hearts of men. It expresses itself in brotherhood, in good will, and in mutual aid. It is the application, in all human relations, of the principle of service.

What has come out of the old world order, we behold every day, in scenes of indescribable horror. Trial and tribulation are fast becoming the lot of all. So much that is precious and good is lost in violent death, and in the welter of destruction. These evil things must not prevail.

While the old order is destroying itself, a new relationship of men and of nations is already beginning its slow but sure evolution. It is based not on fear, on greed, and on hate, but on mutual trust and the noblest qualities of the human heart and mind. It seeks neither to divide nor to destroy. Its aim is brotherhood, its method co-operation.

ONE GREAT BROTHERHOOD

The new order found expression when Britain determined to put an end to aggression in Europe. It expressed itself at the outbreak of war, when this young nation and other nations of the British Commonwealth took their place at the side of Britain, and made a free-will offering of their treasure, and their blood, in the defence of freedom. You will find its latest manifestation in the resolution of the United States of America to lend its powerful aid to the nations which are fighting for freedom.

All these things are combining to create one great brotherhood of the English-speaking peoples. Nations large and small are finding, in its aim, a new unity in the common defence of freedom and human rights. On such a foundation of unity of purpose and of effort, free peoples may well hope to build an enduring new world order.

> "And I saw a new heaven and a new earth: for the first heaven and the first earth were passed away; and there was no more sea . . . and there shall be no more death, neither sorrow, nor crying, neither shall there be any more pain; for the former things are passed away."

A NEW HEAVEN AND A NEW EARTH

A new heaven and a new earth—are not these, in very truth, what we seek to-day? A heaven to which

men, and women and little children no longer will look
in fear, but where they may gaze again in silent worship, and in thankfulness for the benediction of the sun
and the rain; an earth no longer scarred by warfare
and torn by greed, but where the lowly and the humble
of all races, may work in ways of pleasantness, and
walk in paths of peace.

And the sea no longer will be the scene of conflict,
nor harbour any menace; it, too, will gladden the
hearts of men as it unites, in friendly intercourse, the
nations of the world.

> Then, . . . *"shall all men's good*
> *Be each man's rule, and universal Peace*
> *Lie like a shaft of light across the land,*
> *And like a lane of beams athwart the sea,*
> *Thro' all the circle of the golden year".*

This new heaven, this new earth is the vision
which, at this time of war, unites, inspires, and guides
Britain, Canada, and other nations of the British
Commonwealth, and the United States. No lesser vision
will suffice to gain the victory. No lesser service to
humanity will hold the faith and win the gratitude of
mankind.

CANADA'S CONTRIBUTION TO FREEDOM

On March 18, 1941, the government announced that with a view to strengthening the Pacific coastal defences of Canada and the United States, work had begun, in accordance with a recommendation of the Permanent Joint Board on Defence, on the construction of a series of flying fields extending through northwestern Canada to Alaska.

The signature, on March 19, of the Great Lakes-St. Lawrence Waterways Agreement marked a further stage in the development of collaboration for defence, as well as for purposes of economic co-operation, between Canada and the United States.

On March 25, in closing the debate on the resolution which preceded the introduction of the War Appropriation Bill, the Prime Minister gave a broad picture of Canada's war effort, disclosing, in particular, the magnitude of the material contribution, and the contribution in manpower being made by the Canadian people.

CANADA'S CONTRIBUTION TO FREEDOM

THE HOUSE OF COMMONS, MARCH 25, 1941

WE ARE enacting a measure which pledges Canada to the most stupendous effort in our national history. I feel we should not allow the bill to receive its third reading in this House of Commons without giving the fullest possible credit to those who have made the measure possible, and who are bearing the burden of the tremendous task which it imposes, namely, the people of Canada.

There has been far too great a tendency, both in the house and in the press, to speak of what we are doing as the government's war effort. We all know it is something far greater than that; it is Canada's war effort. What is more, it is an effort which is wholly worthy of Canada, and of which every Canadian is entitled to be justly proud.

As a tribute to the people, whom all of us in this chamber represent, I am going to try this afternoon to put that effort in its true perspective; to give a broad picture of what Canada is already doing, and what we have undertaken to do in the coming year.

CANADA'S ARMED FORCES

It is only eighteen months since we entered the war. Yet, in that year and a half, our armed forces have grown to the point where to-day, in the three services, there are a quarter of a million men on active service.

I might add that this figure does not include over 175,000 additional men, enrolled in the reserve army, who are subject to call for the defence of Canada.

A Canadian Army Corps, Canadian destroyers, and Canadian air squadrons are sharing in the defence of Britain. Our navy and our air force are doing their part to keep open the vital sea lanes of the North Atlantic. Canadian garrisons in Iceland, Newfoundland and the West Indies are on guard in the outposts of this continent. Canadian engineers are strengthening the defences of Gibraltar. In recent months we have also sent overseas, hundreds of radio mechanics for vital defence duties with the Royal Air Force.

From the Atlantic to the Pacific, Canada to-day is throbbing with military activity. Soldiers, sailors and airmen are co-operating in the defence of our ports, our coasts and our coastal waters. The Canadian navy, which had only fifteen ships when war broke out, now has over 180. Nearly sixty military training camps are distributed across the country. In these camps, the soldiers in our active army, and the young men called up under the National Resources Mobilization Act to prepare them for the defence of Canada, are now training side by side. Some ninety establishments of the British Commonwealth Air Training Plan are already in operation. In addition, facilities are being provided for training schools of the Royal Air Force under the jurisdiction of Canada's air ministry.

It is for the maintenance and expansion of this military programme that the present appropriation is being voted. The Minister of Finance expects the appropriation to be exceeded, and his best estimate at present is that, in the next fiscal year,

Canada's direct war effort will cost the Canadian people $1,450,000,000.

What I have said up to the present relates to Canada's outright national contribution as a belligerent. It is being paid for in full by the Canadian people. It is not something that has been leased to Britain. It is not something that is being lent to Britain. It is a direct contribution by Canada to the cause of freedom. It represents the freewill offering which our country began to make over a year and a half ago, when this parliament decided that Canada should enter the war at the side of Britain.

Canada: A Major Source of Supply

But Canada has a twofold task in this war. Not only are we sharing as a full partner in the struggle; not only are we, with but one important exception, ourselves bearing the whole cost of equipping, supplying and maintaining our military, naval and air forces at home and overseas, giving of life as well as of treasure, but we are also helping to supply to Britain equipment, munitions and the other essentials of war.

Canada is a major source of supply for Britain. In common with the United States, Canada is an arsenal of democracy. Since the war began, the British and Canadian Governments have undertaken capital advances of over $380,000,000 for the expansion and equipment of Canadian industry. New plants have been built; old plants extended to make the complex instruments of war, many of which were never before made in this country. The creation of a vast new war industry has taken time.

We have every right to take pride in our industrial

expansion. Canadian labour and Canadian industry have responded splendidly. We have been building an aircraft industry from the ground up. We have already built over fifty small naval vessels and more are being built. We are turning out motor transport vehicles at the rate of hundreds a day. We are producing universal carriers, machine guns, trench mortars, bombs for aircraft, great quantities of shells and ammunition, a wide range of chemicals, electrical apparatus and radio equipment, many other types of essential manufactured goods, large quantities of base metals and alloys, and an increased output of steel. We will shortly begin to produce field guns, and before the year ends, naval guns, anti-aircraft and anti-tank guns and infantry rifles. The production of tanks and of cargo vessels is already under way. Plans are also being made to build destroyers in Canada. Such are the highlights of our programme of war production.

The expansion of production has already been reflected in the absorption of between 330,000 and 350,000 additional men in industrial employment since the outbreak of war. Nor must it be forgotten that the armed forces and industry will make additional demands estimated at over 300,000 men in the coming year. Skilled labour and specialized plant facilities will have to be increasingly diverted to the production of vital war supplies. All along the line, Canadian industry has been geared up to make a maximum contribution to the prosecution of the war.

FINANCIAL ASSISTANCE TO BRITAIN

Perhaps the best illustration I can give of the magnitude of the indirect contribution by Canada to the war is to say that, over and above what is being appropriated for our direct war effort, we expect, during the next twelve months, to send to Britain approximately $1,500,000,000 worth of munitions of war, raw materials and agricultural products.

Britain, of course, cannot herself find all the necessary dollars with which to pay for her enormous purchases of Canadian products. For the new fiscal year, Britain's deficit in her balance of payments with Canada is now estimated at over $1,150,000,000. Canada must provide Britain with the Canadian dollars to meet this deficit, either by purchasing Canadian securities now held in Britain, or by the accumulation of sterling balances.

To meet the total burden upon the Canadian people of our direct war effort and our indirect effort in the form of financial assistance to the United Kingdom during the next fiscal year will, according to the best estimates which can now be made, require almost 44 per cent of the national income.

A MAXIMUM EFFORT

These figures may help members of parliament and the people of our country to appreciate what Canada is committed to, and what is meant by the statement that, in our opinion, Canada is making the maximum effort of which this country is capable.

But this is merely the financial side. Let me also make the comparison in terms of human lives. Apart from Canada's material contribution, Canada's men are participating in this war. The quarter of a million Canadians on active service would, in terms of the population of the United States, be equivalent to an armed strength in the forces of the United States of over two and three-quarter million men, and this without taking account of a reserve army for home defence.

For the great contribution which the United States is making; for the still greater contribution which it will make, the government and people of Canada have nothing but admiration and gratitude. Since the United States has pledged its strength to a victorious issue we know that the struggle, though hard, will be shorter. But in the enthusiasm of our satisfaction that the United States has resolved to throw the decisive weight of its material aid into the struggle, we as Canadians have no reason to discount the magnitude of the material contribution and the contribution in man-power which the people of this dominion are making. It should never be forgotten that Canada is spending not only her treasure but her blood. Our eleven million people have given freely and pledged fully their treasure, their resources and their manhood. Canadians, also, have reason to be proud of the part which Canada has had in the reconciliation of the English-speaking peoples, the healing of ancient wounds, and the closing of the great schism of the Anglo-Saxon race.

Surely in the light of such a war record, without boasting and without vainglory, we may all take pride in the vision, the unity, the resolution and the achievement of the Canadian people.

THE INVASION OF YUGOSLAVIA AND GREECE

German penetration into the Balkan peninsula in 1941 kept that part of Europe in a state of acute tension for several months. Roumania, Bulgaria and Hungary successively fell under complete Nazi domination. The same fate appeared to await Yugoslavia when, on March 25, as a result of deceptive diplomacy and overwhelming intimidation, the government of that country adhered in desperation to the axis tripartite pact. As a result, however, of a revolutionary change in the Yugoslav Government which this step precipitated, the Nazi hope of a peaceful conquest was suddenly thwarted. On April 6, a new phase of the war began with an attack by German forces on Yugoslavia and Greece. This new act of aggression marked the beginning on land of the Nazi 1941 military campaign.

THE INVASION OF YUGOSLAVIA
AND GREECE

THE HOUSE OF COMMONS, APRIL 7, 1941

A T DAWN yesterday, the German army and air force launched an attack on both Yugoslavia and Greece. Reports from the fronts are meagre as yet. They are sufficient, however, to make clear that attacks against both countries have been of the ruthless and barbarous character witnessed during the invasion of Poland at the beginning of the war and repeated again against Norway, the Low Countries, and France during the course of the spring campaign of 1940. They mark, in fact, the launching in deadly earnest of the 1941 military campaign.

The world is again witnessing the determination of Nazi Germany to ride roughshod over all countries which dare to oppose the demands of her leaders, or to stand in the way of German domination.

YUGOSLAVIA'S NOBLE RESISTANCE

It appeared as recently as the 26th of March, that Nazi Germany, by a process of intimidation, was about to add Yugoslavia to her already extended list of victims, thereby achieving, through deceptive diplomacy and overwhelming intimidation, another bloodless victory. On the previous day at Vienna, the government of Yugoslavia, in desperation, had adhered to the tripartite pact, signed at Berlin on September 27, last year, by Germany, Italy and Japan, and agreed that Germany might make use of Yugoslav roads and railways in its projected attack on Greece. The pact, however, was never ratified. The mere announcement of its terms provoked widespread resentment in Yugoslavia. Popular opinion made itself so strongly felt that the council of regents, responsible for the country's betrayal, took refuge in flight. The young king, Peter II, assumed the throne, and a new government was formed which soon gained the support of every section of the Yugoslav people. It made clear the determination of the country to maintain its independence. Because of this attempt by Yugoslavia at self-preservation, Hitler is now seeking to gain by violence what he failed to obtain by subtle means.

The courage of the Yugoslav nation is the more heroic in that Germany within the past few months has gained all the advantages of a complete occupation of Roumania and Bulgaria, and is supported in her present onslaught by Italy and by her control of Hungary, each of which countries has had designs on Yugoslav territory. Italy has, in fact, already boasted of attacking Yugoslavia.

The Nazi attempt to subjugate Yugoslavia followed what has come to be the classic Nazi pattern of aggression. Just as Czechoslovakia was half conquered by the occupation of Austria, just as Poland and Hungary were half conquered by the occupation of Czechoslovakia, just as France was more than half defeated by the invasion of the Low Countries, and just as the Nazis hoped by the conquest of Norway and the occupation of France to outflank Britain, so the Nazis expected that the outflanking of Yugoslavia by the occupation of Roumania and Bulgaria would serve to undermine the spirit of resistance in the Yugoslav people. The Nazis expected that, almost surrounded, Yugoslavia would consider resistance hopeless and surrender without a struggle. The action of Yugoslavia in offering resistance in the face of well-nigh overwhelming odds has undoubtedly come as a surprise to Germany.

GREAT TRADITIONS HONOURED

Throughout their troubled history, the Yugoslavs have given proof on a hundred battlefields of great military virtues and of a stubborn courage in the face of heavy odds. Their determination to resist this latest act of brutal aggression, to fight, and if need be to die in order to preserve their homeland and their hard-won liberties, opens a chapter, however tragic, which does the highest honour to their great traditions. A reversal of policy so sudden and complete as that witnessed in the case of the Yugoslav administration in the past few days is rare indeed, even in a generation which has become accustomed to kaleidoscopic changes. The Yugoslavs, however, to cite as examples only their immediate neighbours, had before them the fate of Hungary, of Roumania and of Bulgaria. One by one these countries in turn, having yielded to a succession of threats, first economic and then military, have found themselves in the end the victims of German aggression. Whatever form the so-called co-operation took, in practice it was discovered to mean the occupation of their territory by Nazi forces, and a complete submission to Nazi domination in economic, political and military spheres. All three countries ceased to be the masters of their own destinies and became the tools of German policy. This fate the Yugoslavs were determined to avoid, if at all possible, at however great a cost.

In Yugoslavia's noble resistance, Nazi diplomacy suffered a signal defeat. In her attempt to subjugate the Balkan peninsula, Germany has been forced to fight. War on two fronts, the spectre which long has haunted German strategy, has become a grim reality. To what lengths the new front may extend, to what proportions the war itself may grow, time alone will disclose.

INDOMITABLE COURAGE OF GREECE

The Nazi attack is directed mainly at Greece as the key to the situation in the eastern Mediterranean. Having voluntarily met the attacks of Germany's ally for five long months, after having inflicted heavy losses upon the Italian invaders and driven them from Greek soil, Greece has now to face the force of Nazi Germany herself, on another and more exposed section of her extended frontiers. It is a tremendous task: in terms of military equipment and power, one that would seem to be almost overwhelming. Greece, however, has revealed that a heroic spirit is more to be desired than all else. The Greeks have already risen to face their new enemy with indomitable courage and with the united will of the whole Greek nation.

The Nazi attack on Yugoslavia and Greece is a

major development.   It is too early even to surmise
what it may portend.   We must be prepared to witness
a stupendous conflict.   We should realize, too, that the
Nazi design of conquest in the Balkans is not an end
in itself.   It is another attempt at outflanking positions
which are obstacles in the path of world domination.
Each country Germany occupies serves two purposes:
the resources of the conquered people are added to her
strength, and a new base is acquired for the next act
of aggression.   Germany is seeking the subjugation
of the Balkan peninsula as a step in the outflanking
of Britain's position in the Mediterranean.

A Symbol of Ultimate Victory

In the whole situation, however, nothing could be
more significant than that at last the great Nazi military machine has not been able to impose the Nazi will
by threats, fear and intimidation.   That is in itself
symbolic of ultimate victory.   The feeling of hope and
encouragement it affords should not, however, blind
us to the realities of the situation.   The great Nazi
army is still intact, and still undefeated; it outnumbers
the Greek and Yugoslav armies many times over.   The
aid which can be sent to these two countries is necessarily restricted.   Moreover, the Balkan peninsula is
not the only or even the major theatre of war.   Indeed
the opening of the Balkan campaign may well be the
prelude to a great battle for the whole Mediterranean
basin.   The Nazis had hoped that a bloodless conquest
would secure their supplies from the Balkan region
and bring them a step nearer to the consolidation of
the whole of continental Europe as a Nazi stronghold.

We can all be profoundly grateful that in the Nazi path, Greece and Yugoslavia have become active obstacles.

In a world struggle events must be viewed in perspective. The conflict must be seen as a whole. Facile optimism and exaggerated expectations may be just as dangerous as abject fear. We must be prepared in the new phase of the war which has now actively begun for a bitter struggle. In the end, the spirit of freedom will conquer. Meanwhile, there is certain to be frightful destruction of life and property, and we must be prepared for set-backs and disappointments. The heroism of the Greeks and the determination of the Yugoslavs may well fill with fresh courage all of those who love liberty.

THE CONFLICT IN THE MIDDLE EAST

The main development of the war, during the Easter recess of parliament, was the Nazi conquest of Yugoslavia and Greece. When the House of Commons renewed its sittings, on April 28, the Prime Minister reviewed the momentous events of the preceding weeks. In relating Germany's ambition with respect to the Mediterranean as the key to the domination of the rest of continental Europe, of the Middle East, and of North Africa, he availed himself of the occasion to prepare the country for rapidly growing intensity and ferocity of warfare, and the extension of fighting over wide and ever wider areas.

THE CONFLICT IN THE MIDDLE EAST

THE HOUSE OF COMMONS, APRIL 28, 1941

I N YUGOSLAVIA, the familiar pattern of the Nazi blitz-
kreig was repeated. It was Norway, Holland and
Belgium over again. Without pre-arranged plans,
British aid was necessarily less than might otherwise
have been furnished, and also less effective when supplied. While greater aid might have prolonged the
campaign, it is, however, only too true that it could
scarcely have changed the result.

In carrying on by themselves, in Greece and Albania,
the fight against their Italian aggressors, the Greeks
had ever present, to their minds, the necessity of avoid-
ing, if possible, a German attack upon Greece. During
many months of Balkan intrigue there was the prospect that such an attack might come, but there was
also the hope that it might be avoided. It was not until
the German attack appeared inevitable that British
military assistance was accepted. The plain fact is
that the heroic Greeks, as long as Italy was the only
nation in arms against them, gravely resolved, and
magnificently succeeded, in fighting their own battles.

The story of the battles recently fought by the forces
of Australia, New Zealand and Great Britain, and the
final result of their re-embarkation to new battle
grounds, is not yet fully known. It can be said, however, that one of the great actions of military history
has been fought with superb courage. It is with a sense

253

of proud kinship with her sister nations in the British
Commonwealth, that Canada records her admiration
of the daring and bravery of the Australian, New
Zealand and British forces who fought for freedom in
the mountains and valleys of Greece.

SIGNIFICANCE OF LOSSES AND GAINS

Although resistance to the Nazis in the Balkans was
not successful, it would be wholly wrong to imagine
that, by fighting, nothing has been achieved for the
allied cause. The alternative was a bloodless Nazi conquest. The Nazi losses in men and material have certainly been great. But that is not all. The devastation
of Yugoslavia and Greece also marks loss for the Germans. The Nazis had hoped to be able to exploit those
countries as they have exploited Roumania. That
Yugoslavia and Greece proved to be obstacles in the
Nazi path certainly made the way harder for the Nazi
war machine. Above all else, the resistance of these
two peoples obliged Hitler materially to alter his general plan of campaign.

Germany has gained important military objectives,
but her armies and air forces have suffered heavy
losses. For the Italians, the Balkan campaign brought
only defeat to their forces, and national humiliation.
For Britain, the campaign has had some quite definite
advantages. Germany's preoccupation in Roumania,
Bulgaria, Yugoslavia and Greece has given Britain
additional time; and time is of the essence of this phase
of the war, when British resistance and American help
are the implacable powers over which Germany must
triumph if Hitler is to impose his will upon the world.

Apart from tangible and material things, there is ever present the conviction that every time there is heroic resistance against great odds, every time men steel their hearts to preserve a nation's soul, the legions of freedom advance. It has often been said that, in the last analysis, the character of free peoples will decide the issue. Who will say that the heroism of Greece, the honour of Yugoslavia, and the dauntless spirit of Britain and the British dominions have not served to maintain the morale of the world?

The Control of the Mediterranean

It would be unwise to minimize the added danger to Alexandria, Suez and Haifa of the presence of Nazi forces in Libya, or the demonstration of the ability of the enemy to move his forces to North Africa. While events have shown that naval power is the most effective British weapon in the present Libyan campaign, sight must not be lost of the fact that a fleet cannot continue to operate without bases or without an assured fuel supply.

The growing unrest in Iraq, Syria and the Arabian desert is a threat to the oil supplies of the British Navy in the Mediterranean. It was to defend her communications and her vital oil resources that Britain recently landed troops at Basra in the Persian gulf. We should not overlook the fact that the threat to British interests in Iraq is also a menace to Turkey. The now familiar Nazi technique is, once more, in evidence. Instead of making a frontal attack, Hitler, clearly, is seeking to outflank and isolate the Turks. The success of this movement would mark the realization of the "Berlin-to-Bagdad'' dream of the Germans in 1914, and would open to German exploitation the great oil fields of Mosul.

The enemy is not limiting his interest to the eastern Mediterranean. The presence of a Nazi force in Libya also constitutes a potential threat to the French possessions in North Africa. By turning westwards, the Nazis might use their force in Libya as the left flank of a pincer movement directed against Gibraltar, which is already menaced by the Nazi army in the Pyrenees, ready, if a chance offers, to strike through Spain.

The Germans obviously regard the control of the Mediterranean as the key to the domination of the rest of continental Europe, of the Middle East, and of North Africa. British naval power in that sea remains the most formidable obstacle to Nazi ambition. Realizing the impossibility of defeating the navy in open combat on the waters of the Mediterranean, the Nazis are evidently seeking to effect their end by encircling the fleet, cutting its line of communications both at Gibraltar and Suez, and gaining control of its supplies of fuel.

Let me add this: the Nazi design in the Mediterranean is, again, not merely an end in itself. It is another stage in Germany's plan to achieve world domination. A Nazi drive to the Persian Gulf might, if concerted with military action in southeast Asia, constitute a vast axis pincer movement against the whole continent of Asia. In estimating all possible contingencies, we cannot, amid the uncertainty of rapidly moving events, ignore the possibility of an attack on

Singapore taking place at the same time as attacks on Gibraltar and Suez, and an attempted invasion of Britain. We must never forget that the destruction of the British Empire is the supreme aim of the enemy. The world-wide threat to Britain is the measure of the magnitude of her task.

PROBABILITIES BECOME STERN REALITIES

While events have been proceeding with dramatic suddenness in the Balkans, Africa, and the Middle East, the Nazi air attacks over Britain have been intensified, and the grim battle of the Atlantic has not lessened in seriousness.

As respects the Far East, probably the most significant event was the recent visit of the Japanese foreign minister, Mr. Matsuoka, to Berlin, Rome and Moscow, and the signing at Moscow, on April 13, of the Neutrality pact by the Soviet Union and Japan. What these events really signify remains a matter of speculation. The growing tension in the Far East was reflected in the announcement, on April 24, of the landing of another contingent of Australian troops at Singapore.

What have for long been ominous probabilities, are, now, upon us as stern realities. The area of conflict widens every day; its intensity increases every day; losses on sea, in the air and on land will continue to mount; the scenes of terror and destruction which live in the memories of many lands free, beleaguered and invaded, will be repeated and renewed. In steadiness of heart, of hand and of vision we shall find our present strength and the path to victory.

It is of the utmost importance that we should view

the whole struggle in perspective, and seek to preserve a true sense of proportion. We must be prepared for the extension of fighting over wider and wider areas, for a rapidity of movement at times, and in other places, not unlike what we have already witnessed in the Balkan campaign; and for an intensity and ferocity of warfare resulting in terrific destruction and in heavy losses of human life. Regardless of where the conflict may spread or how rapid may be the movement of forces, or how intensive and destructive the struggle may become in other parts of the world, we must keep ever in our mind the truth that so long as Britain stands no reverse will be decisive.

Britain is fighting with every ounce of her strength, every fibre of her being. We, in Canada, will strive more earnestly than ever to do our utmost on sea, in the air and on land; and to work, to produce and to manufacture, as we have never worked and produced or manufactured before. The news received yesterday of the landing in Britain of further contingents of Canadian troops, and airmen trained in the great Commonwealth Plan, should increase our confidence in the ability of Canada to help effectively in the decisive struggle. For the world it is renewed evidence of Canada's determination to spare neither her material resources nor her manhood in the battle for the world's freedom.

CO-OPERATION IN ECONOMIC DEFENCE —THE HYDE PARK DECLARATION

Parliament adjourned for Easter on April 8, 1941. The Prime Minister availed himself of the recess to visit the President of the United States, and to discuss with Mr. Roosevelt some of the problems arising out of Canada's war-time economic relations with the United States and with the United Kingdom.

At the close of the visit, the President and the Prime Minister issued a joint statement at Hyde Park, New York, on April 20th, 1941. The statement constitutes a reciprocal agreement. It set forth means whereby additional exchange was to be made available for the purchase of war supplies, also the means by which for their production the most prompt and effective utilization was to be made of the existing facilities in the two countries. This statement has come to be known as the Hyde Park Declaration. Its provisions and international significance were explained by the Prime Minister to parliament when the House of Commons resumed its sittings on April 28.

CO-OPERATION IN ECONOMIC DEFENCE—
THE HYDE PARK DECLARATION

THE LEND-LEASE ACT settled the principle of United States assistance to Britain and the other democracies. It did not, however, solve all of the complex economic problems involved in the mobilization of the resources of the United States and Canada in order to render to Britain, in the speediest manner, the most effective assistance and support.

One of the reasons for my recent visit to the United States and my conferences with the President, was the urgent need for Canada to find an immediate solution of some of the problems involved in our war-time economic relations with the United States and with the United Kingdom.

THE WAR EXCHANGE PROBLEM

It will be readily recognized that we, in Canada, could not possibly have embarked upon our existing programme of war production if we had not lived side by side with the greatest industrial nation in the world. Without ready access to the industrial production of the United States, and particularly the machine tools and other specialized equipment so necessary in producing the complex instruments of modern war, Canada's war effort would have been seriously retarded. We would have been forced to embark upon the production of many articles which, because of limited demand, could only have been produced at high cost, and over a considerable period of time. Canada also lacks certain essential raw materials which must be procured from the United States. Since the outbreak of war, we have steadily expanded our purchases in the United States of these essential tools, machines and materials which were required both for our own Canadian war effort, and in the production of war supplies for Britain.

Even in normal times Canada purchases much more from the United States than we sell to our neighbours. In peace-time we were able to make up the deficit by converting into United States dollars the surplus sterling we received as a result of the sale of goods to Britain. But from the outset of war, this has been impossible. The government realized at once that Canada would be faced with a growing shortage of United States dollars to pay for our essential war purchases. To conserve the necessary exchange the Foreign Exchange Control Board was established on September 15, 1939. As the need has grown, increasingly stringent measures have been adopted to reduce the unessential demands for United States dollars in order to conserve sufficient funds to make our payments for essential weapons and supplies of war. These war purchases could not be reduced without a corresponding, or perhaps an even more serious reduction in our war effort. Despite the drastic measures taken to conserve exchange, the lack of United States dollars was becoming, as one writer expressed it, one of the most serious "bottlenecks" in Canada's war effort.

RISK OF WASTEFUL DUPLICATION OF PRODUCTION

The problem of exchange was the most urgent problem we faced in our economic relations with the United States. But we also realized a growing danger of possible unnecessary duplication of production facilities on the North American continent, with consequent undue pressure on scarce labour and materials if Canada and the United States each tried to make itself wholly self-sufficient in the field of war supplies. We felt it imperative to avoid such waste, which might well have had the most serious consequences. The experience of the Department of Munitions and Supply, and the studies of the Permanent Joint Board on Defence, both suggested the same solution. That solution was the co-ordination of the production of war materials of Canada and the United States. This was in reality a simple and logical extension, to the economic sphere, of the Ogdensburg Agreement.

The practical experience of a year and a half of organizing and developing war production in Canada revealed that many of the essentials of war could be made in the comparatively small quantities required by Canada only at a prohibitive cost. They could, however, be produced economically in the United States where the demand was large enough to result in the economies of large-scale production. On the other hand, the production of other weapons and materials had been developed in Canada to the point where output could be expanded more quickly, and probably more economically, than new production facilities could be organized in the United States. It was, therefore, only common sense to extend to the production of war materials the same reciprocity in which, at Ogdensburg in August last, our two countries had permanently placed their defence.

THE HYDE PARK DECLARATION

During my Easter visit, I had the opportunity of preliminary discussions with the Secretary of State, Mr. Cordell Hull, and the Secretary of the Treasury, Mr. Morgenthau, at Washington. I also, later, had an opportunity of conferring with Mr. Harry Hopkins, who has been entrusted with immediate direction and supervision of the measures to be taken under the Lend-Lease Act. On Sunday, April 20, I spent the day with the President at Hyde Park. At the close of the visit, I gave to the press a statement of the understanding which the President and I had reached regarding the problems I have mentioned. That statement it is proposed to call the Hyde Park Declaration.

The Declaration reads:

"Among other important matters, the President and the Prime Minister discussed measures by which the most prompt and effective utilization might be made for the productive facilities of North America for the purposes both of local and hemisphere defence, and of the assistance which in addition to their own programme both Canada and the United States are rendering to Great Britain and the other democracies.

"It was agreed as a general principle that in mobilizing the resources of this continent each country should provide the other with the defence articles which it is best able to produce, and, above all, produce quickly, and that production programmes should be co-ordinated to this end.

"While Canada has expanded its productive capacity manifold since the beginning of the war, there are still numerous defence articles which it must obtain in the United States, and purchases of this character by Canada will be even greater in the coming year than in the past. On the other hand, there is existing and potential capacity in Canada for the speedy production of certain kinds of munitions, strategic materials, aluminium and ships, which are urgently required by the United States for its own purposes.

"While exact estimates cannot yet be made, it is hoped that during the next twelve months Canada can supply the United States with between $200,000,000 and $300,000,000 worth of such defence articles. This sum is a small fraction of the total defence programme of the United States, but many of the articles to be provided are of vital importance. In addition, it is of great importance to the economic and financial relations between the two countries that payment by the United States for these supplies will materially assist Canada in meeting part of the cost of Canadian defence purchases in the United States.

"In so far as Canada's defence purchases in the United States consist of component parts to be used in equipment and munitions which Canada is producing for Great Britain, it was also agreed that Great Britain will obtain these parts under the Lend-Lease Act and forward them to Canada for inclusion in the finished articles.

"The technical and financial details will be worked out as soon as possible in accordance with the general principles which have been agreed upon between the President and the Prime Minister."

Purpose and Principle of the Declaration

The immediate purpose of the joint Declaration is set out in its first paragraph, which might be described as the preamble. It states that the President and I discussed measures by which the most prompt and effective utilization might be made of the productive facilities of North America. Let me emphasize the two words: prompt and effective. They indicate that, while recognizing the short-run necessity of speed, the vital importance of the time factor, we have not lost sight of the long-run necessity of the utmost efficiency in the organization of our war production.

The preamble goes on to recognize a twofold object in ensuring this prompt and effective utilization of the productive facilities of both countries. Not only does it envisage the extension of the scope of our joint defence arrangements to the economic sphere, but is recognizes the advantages of co-ordinating the use of the resources of both countries as a means of speeding up and increasing the volume of aid to Britain from this continent.

Let me state this in another way. The Hyde Park Declaration is more than an extension of the Ogdensburg Agreement for hemispheric defence. It is also a joint agreement between Canada and the United States for aid to Britain. It constitutes an acceptance of the economic inter-dependence of Canada and the United States as the foundation of the programme of war production in both countries. It represents the application to war production of the principle, recognized by Canada and the United States in the trade agreements of peace time, that the exchange of goods is of mutual benefit.

PRACTICAL OPERATION OF THE AGREEMENT

One question which may arise in connection with the Hyde Park Declaration is: how can Canada spare to the United States any defence articles or munitions? Surely, it will be said, all our war production is needed either for Canada or for Britain! The answer is that we have advanced so far in the production of certain articles that expansion beyond British and Canadian needs can be readily accomplished. That is true of certain types of small arms, guns and ammunition, certain explosives and chemicals, certain armed fighting vehicles, aluminium and certain other metals and materials, merchant ships and naval vessels of the type we have been building, namely, corvettes and mine-sweepers. There are in addition certain types of clothing and textiles, certain leather, rubber and timber products, and certain secret devices in which Canada could probably make an important contribution, if these were desired. On the other hand, the production of engines for aircraft in Canada would be a slow process, costly both in time and in those types of skilled labour and specialized equipment of which no surplus exists. Moreover, this is a field in which not one but many types are needed to fill the varied demands and improvements in designs that are constantly occurring.

The fact that Canadian war production is so well organized in many fields as to enable Canada to meet speedily many United States requirements is a high tribute to Canadian industry and Canadian labour.

While these United States purchases will assist us very materially in meeting our deficit, they alone will not solve the whole problem. A further important contribution to its solution is contained in another paragraph of the Declaration which provides that Canadian purchases in the United States of materials or components to be used in equipment and munitions being produced by Canada for Britain will be made available to Britain under the terms of the Lend-Lease Act. Hitherto it has been necessary to Canada to find United States dollars to pay for these purchases on British account. These purchases have materially added to the growing deficit in our balance of trade with the United States.

The combination of United States purchases in Canada and the lease-lending of defence articles for Britain will go a very long way toward the solution of Canada's acute exchange problem.

Far-reaching Significance of the Declaration

The most immediate significance of the Hyde Park Declaration is that, through the co-ordination of war production in both countries, it will result in the speeding up of aid to Britain by the United States and Canada. As a result of the better integration of North American industry, the proposed arrangement will, through increasing total production, have the further effect of increasing the total volume of aid to Britain. It will have a corresponding effect upon Canada's war effort. Full utilization of the production facilities we have built up, and specialization on those things which we are best fitted to produce, will increase both our national income and our own armed strength, as well as increasing our capacity to aid Britain.

Beyond its immediate significance, the Hyde Park Declaration will have a permanent significance in the relations between Canada and the United States. It involves nothing less than a common plan of the economic defence of the western hemisphere. When we pause to reflect upon the consequences, in Europe, of the failure of the peace-loving nations to plan in concert their common defence, while yet there was time, we gain a new appreciation of the significance for the future of both Canada and the United States of the Ogdensburg Agreement and of this new Declaration which might well be called the economic corollary of Ogdensburg.

For Canada, the significance of the Hyde Park Declaration may be summarized briefly as follows: first, it will help both Canada and the United States to provide maximum aid to Britain and to all the defenders of democracy; second, it will increase the effectiveness of Canada's direct war effort; and finally, through the increased industrial efficiency which will result, it will increase our own security and the security of North America.

The utmost effort of the Canadian people is more than ever needed in the present phase of this terrible struggle; but in making that effort we shall have, as the result of the agreement, the added satisfaction of knowing that we are making a greater contribution than otherwise would be possible to the cause of freedom.

Last November, I said that the link forged by the Ogdensburg Agreement was no temporary axis, formed by nations whose common tie was a mutual desire for the destruction of their neighbours. The Hyde Park Declaration is, I believe, a further convincing demonstration that Canada and the United States are indeed laying the enduring foundations of a new world order, an order based on international understanding, on mutual aid, on friendship and good will.

TILL THE HOUR OF VICTORY

During the month of June, the Canadian people were asked, in support of Canada's war effort, to subscribe to the largest public loan ever sought by the dominion. The loan, which was the third of Canada's war loans, was described as the 1941 Victory Loan. The campaign was opened on June 1 by the Prime Minister, speakin English, and the Rt. Hon. Ernest Lapointe, Minister of Justice, speaking in French. The Prime Minister's address took the form of a message which was broadcast to the people of Britain. It was replied to in a broadcast to the Canadian people by the Prime Minister of Great Britain.

The symbol of Canada's united national appeal was a Victory torch. The torch after being flown in the course of the campaign from the Pacific coast to the Atlantic, was, upon the successful completion of the campaign, borne across the sea by Hon. Ian Mackenzie, Minister of Pensions and National Health, and presented to Mr. Churchill as a symbol of the spirit of the Canadian people, and their determination to share Britain's burdens till the hour of victory.

Hon. C. G. Power, Minister of National Defence for Air, also visited the United Kingdom during the month of July for purposes of Conference.

TILL THE HOUR OF VICTORY

BROADCAST, JUNE 1, 1941

THE heart of Canada has been deeply touched by what the people of Britain have been called upon to bear. We have felt deeply for you in the loss of your loved ones and your homes. Your losses and your sufferings have drawn us closer to your side in sympathy for your grief, and in admiration of your endurance.

We understand the agony of human sacrifice. We know, too, how through separation, anxiety is increased and grief intensified. Our minds have been stricken with horror at the brutal bombing of innocent babes and little children, of men and women at their daily tasks, of the sick, the aged and the infirm.

We also know something of the spiritual values which attach, through association, to material things. For us, the Houses of Parliament, Westminster Abbey, St. Paul's, the national monuments, the historic churches and homes of Britain are a part of our heritage in the British Commonwealth. Their wanton destruction has deepened our resolve to defend the spiritual inheritance of which your ancient buildings are an outward sign.

Above all, we have been inspired by your bravery, your undaunted courage, your determination to fight to the end, that the flag of a free people may never cease to fly over the citadel of the world's freedom.

Let me tell you, too, what the example of King George and Queen Elizabeth has meant to us. In their visit to Canada, Their Majesties became very much a part of ourselves. The rejoicings of that Royal Visit still hold their place in our memories. To the love inspired by their presence, we now add our highest admiration for the nobility of soul which we see revealed as Their Majesties, with smiling courage, share, amid scenes of cruel devastation, the dangers and the sorrows of their people. With us, as with you, "God Save the King" has become the people's prayer.

Regardless of fortune or circumstances, you seem, one and all, to be endowed with the same fortitude and the same spirit.

And this leads me to tell you why it is that we in Canada are so completely at one with you in Britain, and so determined to do our utmost for victory.

One in the Love of Liberty

We are not all kith and kin—but as Canadians we are one in our love of liberty. There are no divided loyalties in Canada. Loyalty to Canada, loyalty to the cause of Britain, loyalty to the cause of humanity, these to us have become one and the same.

A century and a half ago, French Canada had already learned the significance of British freedom. Her sons have never forgotten it, and they never will. More than once Canada has been saved to the British Crown by descendants of the men who came to the new world from France.

Many of the newcomers to our land still speak the

languages of foreign motherlands. But even better than other Canadians, they understand the meaning of the evil doctrines of racial hatred and racial superiority. They came to Canada to be free from the continuing menace of international strife, and the debasing fears of an order of society which perpetuates inequality and injustice. Like the early settlers from France and Britain, they have come to this new land, seeking freedom and happiness.

But for freedom to result in happiness, it must be directed aright. I said at the outset of the war, that if I were called upon to sacrifice, out of my life, all save one of the influences of the past, or of present possessions, the one thing I would wish to retain is the influence of the Christian training of my childhood days. That has been a sheet anchor through life. It is this sheet anchor of which the Nazis would rob mankind. They seek to-day, not a heaven, but a hell on earth. There is not one of the ten commandments, not one of the beatitudes in the Sermon on the Mount, against which they have not blasphemed. They have taught youth to hate and despise the very things we cherish most. Hitler and his Nazi associates speak of a new order! What kind of world can come out of any order controlled by such men?

We have never mistaken the real issue. When war came, we, like you, had come to see that to preserve Christian civilization, men must be prepared to lay down their lives. Our armed forces, like yours, are the defenders of freedom; like yours, they are equally defenders of the faith. And that is why we began by sending you men, as well as weapons and munitions.

That is why, changing our national economy from one of peace to one of war, our armed forces on land, at sea, and in the air, have grown in numbers, as we have increased the output of war supplies. Our whole war effort, in men and materials alike, has steadily gained in momentum, in volume, and in power.

SHARING BURDENS

For twelve months you have borne the brunt of the enemy's attacks. Your towns, your ports, your workshops, and your homes, are still his main target. Every month, from now on, as in the past, will see more Canadians with you to share in your defence.

Ever since your shores were threatened, Canadian soldiers have stood on guard with yours prepared to drive back the invader. Impatient at times, that they have not come to grips with the foe, we and they are nonetheless proud that they have been given the high duty and the grave responsibility of sharing in the defence of Britain itself. As the Canadian Corps Commander, General McNaughton, has pointed out, theirs it is to help garrison the one vital citadel, the retention of which decides the war. You know that they are ready to go and that we are equally ready to have them go, wherever their service may count for most. During the present year, we shall despatch to Britain a third infantry division, a tank brigade, an armoured division and many re-inforcements, all equipped and maintained at our own expense.

Ships of Canada's navy have, as you know, been engaged with your ships in the coastal waters of Britain. Other Canadian ships are taking their part in

the duties of convoy on the great passageway of the
Atlantic, so vital, not only to the present of Britain,
but also to the future of Canada and of the United
States of America.

Canadian air squadrons, too, have been taking their
part in the battle of Britain. In the Royal Canadian
Air Force we have to-day 50,000 men. Every day that
valiant brotherhood receives many new comrades in
the proud partnership we enjoy with Australia, New
Zealand and the United Kingdom in the British Commonwealth Air Training Plan.

In this land of great horizons, clear skies and wide
spaces, over 90 training establishments are already in
full operation. From this source is flowing to Britain
an ever-growing stream of pilots, observers and gunners. They are already crossing in thousands and will
continue to come to you in ever increasing numbers.

"England, so long the mistress of the sea,
　Where winds and waves confess her sovereignty,
　Her ancient triumphs yet on high shall bear,
　And reign, the sovereign of the conquered air."

In this war of machines, we are making machines of
war for you, as well as for ourselves. We will also
continue to send you all the food which ships can be
found to carry. But we will not stop there. We
recognize the tremendous financial burden you are
bearing. That burden as well we are ready to continue
to share in increasing measure.

Marshalling the Forces of Freedom

In conclusion, may I send to you, Mr. Churchill,
warmest greetings and remembrances of what to me

has been a valued friendship of many years. It is a proud privilege, indeed, to share with you some of the responsibilities and burdens of a people's trust. To us you are the personification of Britain in this her greatest hour. Your noble words, your high courage, your inflexible resolve, have been an inspiration and a tower of strength. Our citizens, English-speaking and French-speaking alike, and all who have come to us from other lands, hail you as the captain of the great host of free men. Your gallant leadership is marshalling the forces of freedom throughout the world. May God continue to give to you, the strength, the vision and the wisdom so greatly needed in so great a task.

CHANGING PHASES OF WORLD-WIDE WAR

Parliament adjourned on June 14, 1941. The day before the adjournment, the Prime Minister gave the House of Commons a brief appreciation of the war situation as existing at the time. He also gave, in briefest outline possible, a statement of the contribution being made by Canada towards the winning of the war.

CHANGING PHASES OF WORLD-WIDE WAR

THE HOUSE OF COMMONS, JUNE 13, 1941

W HETHER it is better to fight and lose, or not to fight at all, is one of the oldest questions facing military strategists confronted with an enemy of superior strength. Reverses there are bound to be, and we must not lose heart when they come. In an attempt to capture the changing phases of a worldwide war, it is obvious that the picture, if relieved by sunshine, must also be darkened by shadow. To-day there may be an encircling gloom—to-morrow there will be shafts of light.

When we recall that up till a year ago Britain placed her main reliance on the French forces in Syria and North Africa and on the French fleet in the Mediterranean for the protection of the common allied interests in the whole Mediterranean basin, and then reflect that a year has passed since the collapse of France and no vital British position has yet been lost, it should give us cause, not for satisfaction certainly, but at least for thankfulness.

A Long, Grim Struggle

No thoughtful man could ever have believed that this war would be over in a few months, or won by a short, sharp thrust. From the very beginning it was obvious that the volcanic forces let loose in the world were so mighty that a long, grim struggle was inevitable. It was bound to spread from nation to nation, from ocean to ocean, and from continent to continent. The weak, the unprotected, and the perversely neutral were obliged to fall by the wayside. The final conflict was inevitably destined to be waged between the strong. To-day, in what may be the bitterest chapter of the battle for freedom, state discipline fights self-discipline. The strongest men ever forged and hammered by a state meet on many fronts the strongest men ever tempered by the fires of liberty.

In this chapter a few indubitable facts stand out in bold relief. The war will be won or lost not in Africa or in Asia or in the islands of the Pacific, but in the wide waters of the Atlantic, on the shores and in the skies of Britain. The Mediterranean is but an outskirt of the city of liberty. The battlements are in the Atlantic and the English Channel. Freedom falls only if Britain falls.

Let me for a moment seek to balance our advantages and our disadvantages in the air, on the land and at sea.

THE WAR IN THE AIR

In the air, the balance of machine power is gradually being adjusted. Increasing numbers of Nazi bombers are being destroyed at night; British raids on German objectives have not only grown more effective, but no longer can the official silence of the usually over-loquacious German propaganda ministry hide their results from the German people. In his Reichstag speech on May 4, Hitler was forced to promise still better weapons next year. This statement was the first indication given to the German people that the war would not, as hitherto forecast by Hitler, be ended this year. Thus are the prophecies of the violent put to confusion by free men.

The stream of machines continues to flow. If any further evidence were needed of the growth of the British and allied air power, it is to be found in aggressive activity in the Atlantic Ocean, in the North Sea and in the Mediterranean. It is to be found too in the steady defensive activity that every day pursues its revenges against those who scatter indiscriminate murder and destruction upon British soil from the British air. Everywhere in sky warfare, a situation, not yet mastered, nevertheless improves from day to day.

THE BATTLE OF THE ATLANTIC

On the sea the curve of loss has recently shown a decline. The shipping losses for May were considerably lower than they were in April. The attack of the *Bismarck* upon H.M.S. *Hood* was followed by relentless pursuit and swift retribution. The reality of British sea power remains.

Most heartening of all in the present situation is the attitude of the United States. The promises of President Roosevelt are not only being kept, they are being enlarged. The announcement by the President on April 29 that United States warships would be sent wherever the needs of hemispheric defence required their presence; the speeches of Mr. Stimson and Mr. Knox early in May; the passage by the Congress of the bill authorizing the seizure of foreign vessels in United States waters; all these were encouraging signs of stiffening opinion. But the decisive point was reached by the President in his broadcast on May 27, when he made it plain that the United States would take whatever steps were necessary to ensure the delivery of American supplies to Britain. Mr. Roosevelt did not minimize the seriousness of the battle of the Atlantic. His statement that British shipping losses far exceeded the present combined shipbuilding capacity of Britain and the United States marks a thoroughly realistic facing of the facts.

This continent is rapidly becoming not only the arsenal of democracy, but the shipyard of the freedom of the seas. Canada has mobilized all possible resources of men, material and suitable location to build ships. American and Canadian construction have begun the race against destruction. Every ship added to the Canadian navy helps to relieve the tremendous burden so gallantly borne by the British Navy. Every new American warship, every new Canadian warship, helps the British Navy to detect and to destroy. Every new merchant ship is a guarantee of men, machines, munitions and food.

MILITARY OPERATIONS ON LAND

In connection with land operations, there is nothing which can be added to the closing remarks of Mr. Churchill made in his speech on Wednesday, June 11. If we eliminate the occupation of the Channel Islands by German forces, at this time of speaking, after nearly two years of war, no enemy soldier has set a foot on British soil. As Mr. Churchill said:

"If anybody had said in June last, we should to-day hold every yard of the territories for which Great Britain is responsible in the Middle East, that we should have conquered the whole Italian empire, that Egypt, Palestine and Iraq would have been successfully defended—anyone who said that would have been thought a foolish visionary. Yet that is the position at the moment."

Those briefly are the salient, they are the outstanding facts about tangible things.

CANADA'S CONTINUING CONTRIBUTION

As far as Canada is concerned, our own war effort in men and materials has steadily gained in momentum, in volume and in power. We are adding every day to the material and strength of the allied cause. Without complaint our people are bearing the heaviest taxes in their history. In addition they are lending their savings to the government. I know that with loyal willingness they will lend and, if necessary, give, whatever is needed to strengthen and supplement the financial resources of the government of this country. The Canadian people are performing a magnificent task. They will not fail the cause to which we have pledged our all. They are producing, and will produce to the limits of their strength and genius, the material, tangible things, without which victory cannot be won.

There remain, also, as our sure strength and shield, the intangible things of the human spirit. The will to live, and to endure every hardship that all may continue to enjoy the blessings of freedom is a part of Canadian character. We in Canada have a veri-

table passion for human brotherhood; a hatred of
hate; an intolerance of intolerance. Ours is the unshaken and unshakable purpose to re-establish upon
the earth, now hideous with the blackened ruins of
civilization, a freedom, wider and more deeply founded
in social and international justice, than ever before
in human history. All these intangible things are the
very fibre and fabric of the national character alike of
the British and Canadian peoples. Tried by many
onslaughts, tested by many defeats, the inner fort-
resses of that character remain unbroken and unbreakable, impregnable, indomitable. Against their walls,
the tides of tyranny and the waves of battle will beat
in vain.

THE UNIVERSITIES—
THE TRUSTEES OF LIBERTY

On June 17, on the occasion of receiving an honorary degree from Princeton University, the Prime Minister spoke at the commencement exercises on the position of the Universities as the guardians of human liberties. He referred to the special need for the recognition of this obligation by the universities of North America in the light of the reactionary tendencies of the day, and the destruction of freedom in Europe and other parts of the world. He brought to the citizens of the United States the friendly greetings of the Canadian people.

THE UNIVERSITIES — THE TRUSTEES OF LIBERTY

ADDRESS, PRINCETON, JUNE 17, 1941

I THANK you, Mr. President, for admitting me to the fellowship of this renowned university. I gratefully accept the distinction. My fellow-countrymen will be quick to recognize it, as I do, as an honour meant for Canada. They will see in it, as I also do, an expression of your abiding pleasure that our two countries, destined by divine Providence to be neighbours, have for so many years lived together in peace and understanding as friends. That pleasure is abundantly shared by the citizens of the Dominion.

Although

"Heaven has shown us separate fires
And our dooms have dealt us differing years."

there is between you and us a community of thought, ideal, and purpose, by which it is ordained that we shall forever walk together as the best of good neighbours. Inspired by the same visions, we seek the same ends.

As with other countries and other peoples, the inner qualities of your nationhood and of our nationhood have not been without their testing in the crucible of pain. With us in bygone years, there were the fires of racial and constitutional strife; with you, the fires of revolution and civil war. We both have partici-

289

pated in other wars. From victory, we each learned magnanimity; from suffering, compassion.

With some falterings, some shortcomings and some failures, we have each in our own way sought to establish the worth of the common man, the dignity of human labour, the equality of human opportunity, the sacredness of human life and the exaltation of our Christian faith. To-day, evil men have placed those precious things in peril. They would change faith, truth and religion, hope and freedom, for unfaith, falsehood, darkness, despair and slavery.

COMMON LOVE OF ETERNAL THINGS

This ceremony to-day seems to me to commemorate our common disdain of the fleeting things that will pass, and our common love of the eternal things that will remain. I see in it also a realization of the kinship between this great university, indeed, between all the universities of this great country, and the universities of Canada.

Universities are the custodians of ideas and ideals which underlie international good will. They express better than any other institutions our common loves and aspirations. Events may alter allegiances but tradition keeps us true to ideas and ideals. Of ideas and ideals which have inspired peoples of British origin, association, and descent, and which have been nurtured by the universities of the Old Land and the New, none has been so powerful in promoting good will between men and nations as that of public service. To the service of Humanity we, as university men, are called and united in a fellowship more ancient and honourable and wider than any other affiliation can promote. By keeping that fellowship unbroken we may well be able to help restore, and to keep unbroken, the peace of the world.

You of Princeton have given to the United States and to the world many famous men. Their labours for human emancipation will grow in the sight of their fellow-men as posterity reaps the harvest of their noble example.

We of the British Commonwealth of Nations are also proud to remember that, among our contributions to Church and State, we gave to Princeton, as one of its Presidents, in the person of Dr. Francis Patton, an illustrious champion of free institutions, and firm defender of the Christian faith. Dr. Patton, as you will recall, was born in Bermuda. He retained his British citizenship throughout. In the years which immediately followed the civil war, when the institutions of learning in the south had not re-opened their doors, he was among a number of earnest young scholars who came to the University of Toronto to pursue their studies. Perhaps I may be pardoned an expression of personal pride if I mention, on this occasion, that no friend of my father was dearer to him than Dr. Patton. During their university days they were close companions. For a time they shared rooms in the same college residence. The name of Dr. Patton and his inspiring friendship came, with the passing of the years, to be honoured and revered by my father's children, no less than by himself.

Time forbids me to speak of other great men asso-

ciated with this university. But there is one whom,
with you, Canada is proud to acclaim to-day. I should
like to mention him particularly.

THE WATCH TOWERS OF HUMAN FREEDOM

Since racial persecution came to curse the land of
Beethoven and Goethe, Princeton has honoured itself,
and the high cause which this university upholds, by
receiving into her midst one who belongs to the saint-
hood of science—Professor Einstein. Were her distinguished sons not so numerous Princeton might well
be content, in these dark and troubled days, to be
remembered for the broad humanity of Woodrow Wilson, his predecessors and his successors; for the sound
scholarship and Christian charity of Patton, and for
the patient search for truth and its triumphant dis-
covery which have distinguished the life of Einstein.

And just because Wilson's humanity, and Patton's
charity, and Einstein's truth have been banished from
many lands the universities of this North American
continent stand more than ever as the watch towers
of human freedom.

A university can only fulfil its true functions in a
society where life is viewed from many sides, and
where social purposes are not single but manifold. Its
influence must languish and die wherever human activity is subordinated to the dictates of the state, and
the enhancement of material power. For, in such a
society, a university becomes a mere training school
where young men chiefly learn how to adapt art for
the deification of a tyrant, and how to apply science
to the upholding of state tyranny.

"Now, God be thanked Who has matched us with His hour."

It is surely the simple truth that, more than ever before, the universities of North America are the trustees of the liberties of man. It is their high privilege to see that no matter what happens elsewhere, truth can here be sought and proclaimed; beauty revered; and the renaissance, not only of learning but of man himself, flower in significance and splendour.

As I stand here to-day and gaze into the faces of those who are about to leave Princeton for the university of the world, and as I recall the other free institutions of learning and enlightenment on this continent, I know in my heart there will be no betrayal of that high trust.

INTERNATIONAL FRIENDSHIP AND GOOD WILL

As I thank you again for the gift which I have received at your hands, may I be permitted to thank you also for the gift which you have bestowed upon one who, an exile from her own country, has honoured Canada by her royal presence. She bears with great courage and dignity the sorrows of her own homeland. She has been welcomed by the citizens of Canada to this continent, which owes so much to the character, the skill and the faith of the people of the country to which she has dedicated her life. The name of the Crown Princess Juliana of the Netherlands will have an abiding place in the chapter of Canadian history which will record the moving events of this war. Canadians will be happy and proud to learn that to-day Princeton has joined with other institutions of learning in this country in making her royal name a part also of American history.

Mr. President, with my thanks, I bring to you and your fellow-citizens of the United States greetings of brotherhood and good will from your northern neighbour. We are grateful for your friendship. We reciprocate it most warmly. We will ever seek to maintain and worthily deserve your confidence and your regard.

CANADA'S WAR EFFORT OUTLINED
IN THE UNITED STATES

Upon the enactment of the Lend-Lease Act, the isolationist minority in the United States began anew the campaign of indirect opposition to the policy of aid to Britain. In this campaign, there were many misrepresentations with respect to Canada's part in the war, and particularly to Canada's financial relations with Britain.

The Prime Minister having received and accepted an invitation to address the Associated Canadian Organizations of New York City on June 17, availed himself of the occasion to speak on Canada's war effort. By a short factual statement of what Canada was actually undertaking in the prosecution of the war, he sought, in an address broadcast throughout the United States and Canada, to remove such erroneous impressions concerning Canada's contribution to freedom as the isolationist campaign had tended to create in the United States.

CANADA'S WAR EFFORT OUTLINED IN THE UNITED STATES

BROADCAST, NEW YORK, JUNE 17, 1941

THE CANADIAN people entered this war of their own free will. As one people, we made the momentous decision by the free vote of a free parliament. Our declaration of war was signed by the King upon the recommendation of His Majesty's Canadian Ministers. The King's proclamation was in the name of Canada. We, in Canada, were as free to make war or to abstain from making war, as the people of the United States are free to make war or to abstain from making war.

The decision of the Canadian Parliament was given as soon after the outbreak of war as parliament could be called together. It was a prompt and united decision. There was no hesitation. There was no compulsion. We knew humanity's crisis was upon us all. We took our stand as a free and independent people who wished to do our utmost to thwart aggression, to maintain freedom, to crush the cursed creed of Naziism, to preclude world domination by any power, and to end forever, if that were possible, the substitution of force for reason as an instrument of national policy.

THE ISSUE

Our people went to war for the sake of Canada, but not for Canada alone. We went to war as well for the sake of Britain, for North American civilization which we are proud to defend, and for the sake of humanity which is above all nations. We saw clearly that Canadian freedom, that North American freedom, was one with British freedom.

We went to war at Britain's side because we believed hers to be the right side. We committed ourselves to her cause because it was our cause—the righteous cause of the liberty of nations, great and small, and of all men, great and humble, rich and poor. If Britain had not been on what we believed to be the side of righteousness, the cause for which she had taken up arms would not have been our cause. I do not hesitate to say that Britain, or no Britain, Canada would never have entered the war if, at the outset, our country had not seen the issue clearly for itself, and believed it to be what all free peoples know it to be to-day.

Canada True to Herself

In our unhesitating decision, and our action which followed, we were true to ourselves. For if any nation was ever inspired by high ideals, unselfish motives and a passion for human freedom and social and national justice, that land was and is Canada. We have a national history without stain of aggression, exploitation, or territorial greed. We have worked always in patience for peace.

In our dealings with other nations, we have been amongst the foremost exponents of conciliation, mediation and arbitration; and the most consistent advocates of international good will and understanding.

We entered this war, we have remained in it, and

shall remain in it till freedom triumphs, because our
people know exactly what the aggression of Naziism
and Fascism means for the future of themselves and
their children. Thousands came as immigrants to our
country, as they did to other parts of this continent,
seeking escape from those evil things, and in the pursuit of peaceful happiness, religious and political freedom, and the right to live out their lives simply and
unafraid.

We are nationally minded, because, as Canadians, we
are free and independent. But we see no escape, no
safety, no refuge in national isolation. We are inter-
nationally minded because our people know that a
threat to freedom anywhere is a threat to freedom
everywhere. We know that there are no longer any
geographical defences strong enough in themselves to
prevent the onset of aggression. We know that tyrannical ambition, once it overleaps itself, will overleap
every boundary whether it be mountain or sea.

NATIONAL UNITY

Knowing these things, and realizing the strength
of the enemy, we entered the conflict—English-speaking Canadians, French-speaking Canadians—as a
united nation. The ancient partnership between
French-speaking and English-speaking Canadians
sealed by the brotherhood of equality and freedom, is
honoured to-day as the unbroken bond of common
patriotic sacrifice. Don't let any one dare to tell you
that French-speaking Canada is not on the side of
freedom in this war. The union of the children of
New France and their English-speaking brothers

which fashioned the Canadian nation remains unbroken and will always so remain.

The generosity of our citizenship into which men of many races have been freely welcomed, has been repaid by unquestioned loyalty to our institutions and our cause.

As soon as the cloud on the horizon, no larger than Hitler's hand, resolved itself into the storm of conflict, we determined that we would not wait until the enemy was at our gates. We went out to meet him at sea, in the air and on land. Against total war, we have brought and shall continue to bring total effort.

Two Major Tasks

For nearly two years, we have been at war. In the war, we have had from the beginning, two major tasks. We continue to play two major parts. Like Britain, we are a nation at war with all the power of our resources, and all the strength of our will. For nearly two years, we have gathered our strength as we have taken our allotted place in the conflict. Our soldiers, our sailors and our airmen are with Britain and her other allies in the front line of battle. Our forces on land, at sea and in the air have been and are being equipped and maintained at our own expense. In addition, like the United States, we are helping Britain by sending to her, to the limit of our capacity, the products of our factories, our farms, our forests and our mines.

The task of arming and fighting as a nation is our own free contribution to the cause of freedom. The task of aiding Britain with munitions and money is an additional effort which Canada is also making for the common cause.

With the United States, and like the United States, we are helping to provide the tools. With Britain and like Britain, we are doing our utmost to help finish the job.

In the nearly two years Canada has been at war, our own effort in men and materials has steadily gained momentum, in volume and in power. Every month sees more Canadian troops, more Canadian sailors and more Canadian airmen added to the number of the defenders of Britain, the defenders of freedom.

Contribution of Man-Power

Let me give you a few figures to show what our nation of 11½ million people has contributed in man-power. In order that their significance may be fully appreciated, let me resolve those figures in terms of the 130 millions who inhabit the United States.

We have in our active armed forces 300,000 men. In comparable figures, the 300,000 men in the army, navy and air forces are equivalent to well over three millions in the armed forces of the United States. We have in the Royal Canadian Air Force, 55,000 men. That number is equivalent to far more than half a million men in the air service of this country.

Service outside Canada in the Canadian army, navy and air force is voluntary. Eighty thousand volunteers are already in Britain. For home defence we have compulsory military service. To-day every able-bodied young men of twenty-one is called up for training for service in Canada for the duration of the war, unless he chooses to enlist for service overseas. Some 170,000 men are enrolled in the reserve army and are subject to call for local defence. In the defence of our Atlantic and Pacific coasts, the army, navy and air force act in close and constant co-operation. Canada's armed forces are sharing, too, in the defence of the island outposts of North America: the West Indies and Newfoundland. For a year, Canadian troops were also stationed in Iceland.

We have, therefore, prepared ourselves for a twofold duty. One duty, as we see it, is to meet the aggressor in the front line of aggression. That is our duty to freedom and humanity. Another duty, which is a part of that already mentioned, is to be prepared to resist the aggressor if he reaches the shores of America. That is a duty we share with the people of the United States. I believe I am not overstating the position when I say that each day helps to make it increasingly clear that what we have done, and are doing for ourselves and for Britain, is likewise a contribution to the defence of the whole western hemisphere.

WAR PRODUCTION

In new factories, in old factories, in converted factories, we are making machines for Britain's armed forces as well as for our own. Canadian motor transport vehicles, machine guns, aircraft, corvettes, minesweepers as well as shells, explosives and chemicals are being sent in growing volume across the Atlantic. We are sending and will continue to send to Britain all the food which ships can be found to carry. We have launched a large merchant shipbuilding programme. Canada, like the United States, is determined that North America will not only be the arsenal of democracy, but also the shipyard of the freedom of the seas.

HYDE PARK AND OGDENSBURG AGREEMENTS

War production in Canada is a partnership between Canada and Britain. Since last April, there has also been a partnership in war production between Canada and the United States. That partnership, I am happy to recall, was established during my last visit to this country, as a result of the agreement reached by President Roosevelt and myself at Hyde Park. I am even happier to reflect that the Hyde Park Agreement is a logical sequel to the far reaching agreement arrived at between the President and myself at Ogdensburg in August last. Under the Ogdensburg Agreement as you are aware, matters pertaining to the defence of the northern half of the western hemisphere became a subject of special study by the Canada-United States Permanent Joint Board on Defence. A major result of the Hyde Park Declaration is that both countries are now in a position to produce more of the weapons and munitions of war, and to produce them more rapidly. This is all-important when time is of the essence of the conflict.

WAR FINANCE

The arming of our country, and the establishment of a great war industry in less than two years, have placed upon the people of Canada a tremendous financial burden.

Our own war effort alone has already cost us more than a billion dollars. Unless that figure is stated in terms of the population and income of the United States, it may sound small in American ears. In those terms, it is roughly equivalent to an expenditure of fifteen billion dollars. In this current year, we expect the cost of our direct war effort to be on a scale equivalent, in United States terms, to between twenty-one and twenty-two billion dollars a year. Every dollar of that is paid by Canada, and is raised in Canada, mainly by taxation.

FINANCIAL AID TO BRITAIN

Canada, in addition, is raising huge sums of money to help Britain. The money is needed to pay for the great quantities of food, raw materials, and war equipment we are sending to Britain on her account. The value of Canadian shipments this year, it is estimated, will reach a billion and a half dollars, or the equivalent of near 23 billion dollars' worth of goods measured in terms of American population and income.

It is not, perhaps, surprising that there should be, in other countries, some persons who do not fully understand what is happening in Canada, and some who do not wish to understand. For example, it has been asserted that Canada is demanding "cash on the barrel-head—for its aid to Britain," that "Canada still sells to Britain for cash at a profit," while the United States is leasing and lending to Britain. Such statements ignore entirely Canada's direct participation in the war at her own expense. They take no account whatever of what we are contributing in human lives, as well as in those material things which it is possible to lease or lend.

If our war effort is to be considered narrowly as a contribution to Britain, rather than broadly what in reality it is—our contribution to the common cause of freedom, then the "cash on the barrel-head" statement overlooks the fact that the whole of Canada's *direct war effort* is a contribution which is neither leased nor lent, but is an out and out free will offering—a gift to the hard-pressed people of Britain, gladly and proudly made, to assist them in maintaining the world's citadel of freedom, and in fighting freedom's battles in other parts of the world.

The "cash on the barrel-head" allegation, the alleged "selling to Britain for cash at a profit," equally misrepresent the nature of Canada's *indirect participation* through financial aid to Britain—the very part, in fact, which parallels, in kind, though not in amount, the lease and lend contribution of the United States.

Canadian producers must, of course, be paid for the goods sent to Britain, just as American producers must be paid. Part of what we send to Britain, Britain pays for in British goods shipped back to Canada. We have reduced our tariffs to make that easier. What good hard cash the British did pay us—in gold—we have had to pay to the United States, along with a great deal of our own gold, for our war purchases in this country.

Apart from British goods sent to Canada, Britain has already needed a billion Canadian dollars to cover her purchases in Canada. About a quarter of this sum Britain paid Canada in gold. It has cost us in the United States more gold than this to enable us to fill our British orders.

The rest of the Canadian dollars Britain needed in Canada, Canada herself has supplied. Some of these dollars were exchanged for Canadian securities held in Britain. The remainder amounts, in effect, to a loan by Canada to Britain.

By far the largest part of the Canadian dollars needed to pay Canadian producers of goods for Britain have been raised and must continue to be raised from the Canadian people in taxes or loans. We have told Britain not to worry about her shortage of Canadian money—that with the enemy at her gates and approaching our shores, there will be time enough to reckon costs and credits once all know that this world is not to be enslaved but free. Meanwhile we will do our best to find, for Britain's Canadian purchases, Canadian dollars, out of Canadian pockets.

TOTAL FINANCIAL COST

It is only when we add together the cost to Canada of our own war activities, and our financial support for Britain, that we reach the total financial burden of war which the Canadian people are shouldering. Translated into comparable American figures, on the basis of our relative populations and incomes, this total burden would amount, within this fiscal year, to something like 35 billion dollars. To carry this load has required very heavy increases in taxes, even on those who are not well off. I am proud to say the Canadian people have willingly accepted this taxation as a part of their contribution to the cause of liberty.

Why Canada is Fighting To-day

We believe that everything which free men value and cherish, on this side of the grave, is in peril in this war. We know that if we lose this fight, all fruits will wither and fall from the tree of liberty. But we shall not lose it. We shall not lose it because the people of Britain stand and will stand in undaunted fortitude and magnificent resistance. We shall not lose it because, although some nations may lie crushed to-day, their souls can never be destroyed. We shall not lose it because we, on this continent of North America, who have been the pioneers of the frontiers of freedom, have already begun to stamp out the prairie fire of tyranny, anarchy and barbarism which every day draws closer to our homes.

For to-day, whether we will it or not, we are all roof watchers and fire fighters. As Canadians, we are proud to fight the flames with the people of Britain who have maintained for free men their faith in freedom, and kept inviolate the majesty of the human spirit.

As Canadians, we are proud of our great and good neighbour, and grateful to know, as all the world knows, that she is with us heart and soul; that her genius, her skill and her strength work against time for those who fight for freedom.

What Canada Seeks to Effect

Some day, peace will crown the sacrifices of all. When that day comes, the peoples of the British Commonwealth and the peoples of the United States will be found at each other's side, united more closely than ever in one great endeavour to undo the wrongs that have been done mankind. For it is, I believe, the unshaken and unshakable purpose of both that there shall be established upon this earth, now so rapidly becoming hideous with the blackened ruins of civilization itself, a freedom wider, and more deeply founded, than ever before in human history.

Surely, we have all come to see that the present conflict is something more than a war between Germany and other powers; that it is "a struggle between permanent and irreconcilable claimants for the soul of man." On the one side stands spiritual freedom, with its high regard for human values, the dignity of manhood, the worth of honest toil, and the sacredness of human personality. On the other side is the spirit of Naziism and Fascism, with their "coarse material standards," their "cult of power and as an end in itself," their "subordination of personality to mechanism," and their "worship of an elaborate and soul-destroying organization." This false and evil spirit has, in our own day, in our own and other lands, permeated all too deeply many phases of social and industrial life. It must be the purpose of our high endeavour to destroy it for all time.

While that work is being done, it will be ours, as well, to do all that lies within us to make supreme upon the earth that friendship, among men and nations, which has ever lain hidden in the heart of mankind.

GERMANY ATTACKS RUSSIA

Early in the morning of June 22, Germany attacked Soviet Russia and the war entered suddenly upon a new and highly significant phase. Nazi leaders immediately sought to create the impression that Germany was defending the world against Bolshevism.

Anticipating this further deception on the part of the Nazis, the Prime Minister, on the evening of the same day, issued a statement concerning Germany's attack upon Russia. It was intended to prevent confusion of the issue in the minds of those strongly opposed to the philosophy of Soviet Russia, and whose fears of the spread of Communism might obscure for them the reality of the Nazi menace. He pointed out that Germany's attack upon Russia had removed the last shadow of doubt concerning Hitler's determination to dominate the world. He welcomed the added strength which Russia would bring to the ranks of those who were fighting to destroy the Nazi menace.

GERMANY ATTACKS RUSSIA

THE GERMAN declaration of war upon Russia constitutes a fresh call to arms throughout the British
Commonwealth. It has removed the last shadow of
doubt, if any yet remained, concerning the purpose of
Hitler to dominate the world.

With a cynicism unequalled in the history of perfidy,
Germany entered into a pact with Soviet Russia, in
order that Russia might be kept inactive until the continent of Europe, including France, was conquered.
That agreement has now been broken with the same
cynicism and perfidy with which it was signed.

Balked in his effort to break the might of Britain,
Hitler has clearly decided to take immediately, instead
of later, another essential step in his march towards
world conquest, namely, the subjugation of Russia.

To-day, Hitler seeks to outflank Soviet Russia
through Finland and Roumania, while delivering a
frontal blow across prostrate Poland. In the Middle
East, he threatens Suez from Greece, from Crete,
and from Libya; at the other end of the Mediterranean, he threatens Gibraltar and its straits, through
infiltration and outflanking in Spain and French North
Africa. From the North Cape of Norway to Cape
Finistère in North-western France, the Nazi forces for
a full year have formed a great half circle around

Britain. Through Russia, Hitler threatens the whole continent of Asia.

If successful in this purpose, the Nazi armies, undisputed masters of continental Europe and a large part of Asia, would then have in their possession vast stores of wheat and oil and munitions of war, for use in a final desperate onslaught against Britain and the western world.

The chief obstacle to Nazi ambitions is still Britain, and Britain can afford to devote but part of her effort to other theatres of war. The threat of invasion of her own island has not passed. The Battle of the Atlantic has not been won.

ULTERIOR DESIGNS IN NAZI ATTACK

The Nazi attack on Soviet Russia is not a crusade against any Red menace. Rather it is a new phase of the attack on Britain and all of the democracies. Should Germany prevail in her campaign against Russia, she would successfully eliminate the threat of war on two fronts. She would leave herself free to concentrate all her forces against Britain and the west.

Hitler's invasion of Russia is also an attempt to deceive and divide the people of the United States and the peoples of the British Commonwealth and their allies. He is again seeking to have it appear that he is the enemy of Bolshevism. Whatever one's opinions may be about the philosophy of the Russian revolution, however strongly some of Russia's international activities may be condemned, to-day, the plain fact is that, as Russia fights Germany, it is not Russia which is a threat to freedom and peace. That threat is Nazi Germany. Indeed one of the effects of Germany's attack on Russia should be to put an end to communistic activities on the part of Russian sympathizers in other lands.

A Time for Unity of Opinion and Effort

The diversion on the eastern front should enable Britain and America to strengthen the western front. No greater error could be made than to suppose that Nazi Germany has abandoned her designs against Britain and the western world. While Russia bears the brunt of the German attack, the Nazi propaganda machine will doubtless seek to beguile the British Commonwealth and the United States into relaxing their efforts. Any weakening of our effort would play right into Hitler's hand. Let us welcome all the help which comes from Russian resistance. But, let us beware the perilous belief that Russia can win the war for us. What we have witnessed of Nazi might since the war began should surely convince us that to win it will take all the strength that can be mustered. It is not a time for less effort, but for more effort. It is not a time, either, for any division of opinion. It is a time for strengthened unity of opinion. The Christian faith, whether it be Catholic or Protestant, depends upon the destruction of Naziism for its survival as a civilizing force amongst mankind. Every force which fights Hitler to-day is fighting consciously or unconsciously, for the preservation of Christian civilization. Every day in which Russian resistance holds German aggression, it is a day contributed to the cause of freedom. It is a day contributed to the might of the combined power of the British Commonwealth and the United States of America.

Let us never forget that the declaration of war on Russia is designed by Germany to make Nazi Germany stronger, and the British Commonwealth of Nations and our allies weaker. We must continue to keep before us the simple truth that everyone who engages our enemy advances our cause. Nor can we afford to forget, as we look across the Pacific, that we also face a continent which for five years has been in arms; and that the most powerful of the warring nations in the East is an Axis partner of Nazi Germany. In whatever direction we look out from the western hemisphere, we see a world ravaged by the fires, torn by the destruction, and convulsed by the horrors of war.

THE WORLD-ENCIRCLING DANGER

Germany's attack upon Russia was a threat from the West to the whole continent of Asia. From the East, fresh dangers began to loom on the Asiatic horizon. A few days before Germany attacked Russia, Japan had broken off trade negotiations with the Netherlands Indies. Immediately after the attack, she began to assert more vigorously her intentions with respect to wider control in the Far East. Whether Japan would employ her armed forces on land and at sea to attack Russia, or to acquire bases in Indo-China and Thailand, or for both these purposes, became a matter of deep concern. The result was a continuing state of acute tension.

On June 24, the Prime Minister began a tour of western Canada. In the course of the tour he visited military, naval and air training establishments, war industries, and Pacific coast defences. He also delivered a series of public addresses. An immediate purpose of the western tour was to assist in a campaign, then in progress, for recruits for the Canadian active army. The addresses included an outline of Canada's war effort. A theme common to all was the world-encircling danger.

THE WORLD-ENCIRCLING DANGER

ADDRESS, WINNIPEG, JULY 10, 1941

I T WILL be recalled that, at the time of the Munich Conference, less than a year before Canada entered the war, Czechoslovakia seemed so remote from Canada that many doubted whether, if war came in Europe, this country would see the danger to its freedom, and the necessity of taking up arms to keep that danger from our shores. The Nazi menace to freedom was widely regarded as something which might increasingly disturb the peace of Europe. It was not seen as something that might come to convulse the world.

The events of the year following Munich helped to make clear the nature and extent of the Nazi threat, and the might and terror which lay behind it. Ere Poland was attacked, thoughtful observers had realized that an ambition much larger than the domination of Central Europe lurked in the mind of Hitler. It was clear that his aim was, at least, the domination of Europe. To-day, we know beyond all shadow of doubt, that aggression in Hitler's mind has no limits. World domination alone will satisfy the ambition of Nazi Germany.

MAGNITUDE OF THE NAZI MENACE

From the very outset of the war, I have sought to keep ever in the public mind the magnitude of the Nazi

menace. I make no apology for repeating to you to-
day what I said, at the outbreak of hostilities, as to the
probable character and scope of the struggle then beginning. You will be surprised, I think, even at this
late date, to see how much of what I then feared and
foretold, has since come to pass.

Speaking at the special session of parliament called
nearly two years ago, to decide upon Canada's entry
into the war, I sought to picture the danger, to Canada
itself, of the conflict which had been commenced in
Europe. To many my words may have seemed unduly
alarming. The unfolding of events has shown that remote as the possibilities appeared, I was not exagger-
ating. I hope that those who are now listening to me
will feel, in the light of what I said then, and what has
happened since, that what I shall say to-day is equally
no exaggeration.

The evening before, I announced in the House of
Commons the government's policy with respect to
Canada's entry into the war at the side of Britain. I
had read a statement of Hitler's to the effect that, if
England wished to fight, she must realize that the prize
of victory would be the British Empire. When I spoke,
I reminded parliament that the British Empire included Canada, and that there was no portion of the
globe which any nation would be likely to covet more
than this dominion.

Let me here repeat what I said in parliament, in
September, 1939.

> "There is," I said, "no other portion of the
> earth's surface that contains such wealth as lies
> buried here. Nowhere are there such stretches of

territory capable of feeding for generations to come —not hundreds of thousands, but millions of people. No, the ambition of this dictator is not Poland. At one time, he said it was only the areas in which there were German-speaking people. But we have seen that ambition grow. That may have been the thought in his mind some years ago, but we all know how ambition feeds upon itself; we all know how the lust for power blinds men's senses to all else.

"We know where and how he started, first with the militarization of the Rhineland. He then said—I quote Hitler's own words—he had 'no thought of annexing Austria.' After giving his word that there would be no further attempt at conquest, he took a part of Czechoslovakia. Then he took Moravia and Bohemia, then Memel, now Danzig and Poland.

" 'Where is he creeping to?'—I am continuing to quote, from the House of Commons debates, what I said at the time—'Where is he creeping to?' I asked. I answered that question in the following words. I ask you to note their significance in the light of what was then deemed impossible, but what since has actually taken place. Where is he creeping to? Into those communities of the north, some of which to-day say they are going to remain neutral. I tell them if they remain neutral in this struggle, and Britain and France go down, there is not one of them that will bear for long the name that it bears at the present time; not one of them. And if this conqueror by his methods of force, violence and terror, and other ruthless iniquities is able to crush the peoples of Europe, what is going to become of the doctrine of isolation of this North American continent? If Britain goes down, if France goes down, the whole business of isolation will prove to have been a mere myth. There will in time be no freedom on this continent; there will in time be no liberty. Life will not be worth living. It is for all of us on this continent,

by helping others, to do our part to save its privileged position.' ''

The Magnitude of the War

We have seen Hitler creep into the communities of
the north, into Denmark and Norway, with his secret
agents, and the saboteurs of his treacherous fifth column. We have watched him spring in the night upon
the peace-loving peoples of Denmark, Norway, Holland
and Belgium, raining indiscriminate destruction from
the skies upon innocent men, women and children. We
have seen France fall. All this came within ten months
of the time at which I spoke. Before, and ever since,
we have watched Britain fighting, month after month,
against terrible odds, for her very life. Less than three
months ago, we witnessed in the course of two short
weeks, the crash of the Nazi hordes through the brave
resistence of Yugoslavia and Greece to the waters of
the Mediterranean, and the attempted invasion of the
Holy Land. Having seen the fate of those who sought
by neutrality to avoid the choice between the destroyers
of freedom and the defenders of freedom; having
watched disaster come to those who sought to stand
aloof; having witnessed the breath-taking ferocity and
rapidity of the march of Nazi conquest, it is hard to
believe that any thoughtful man can longer doubt the
world-encircling scope of Hitler's ambition, and the
appalling reality of the Nazi menace.

To-day, Hitler seeks the conquest of Russia. On the
Mediterranean and in the Middle East, he threatens
Suez from Greece, from Crete, and from Libya; at the
other end of the Mediterranean, he threatens Gibral-

tar and its straits through Spain and French North Africa. Through Russia, Hitler threatens the whole continent of Asia.

The magnitude of the war is matched by the magnitude of its battles. This war began with the battle of Poland. Then came the battles of Norway, of the Low Countries and of France. After that came the first repulse of the enemy in the battle of Britain. To-day the world is in the midst of battles of continents and of oceans: the battle of Asia, the battle of Africa, the battle of the Atlantic. To-morrow may witness the battle of the Pacific.

The Nazi menace is drawing ever closer to this hemisphere. That is the truth I should like to bring home to all to-day. It is a truth which the President and other members of the Administration at Washington are seeking to bring home to the people of the United States, and also to the people of Latin America.

MEANS OF ACCESS TO WESTERN HEMISPHERE

There are two bridges by which Hitler would seek to have his forces penetrate the western hemisphere, once he has consolidated his gains in Europe. The northern bridge extends from Norway, via the Faroe Islands, Iceland, Greenland and Newfoundland to our North Atlantic coasts. It was the possession of that bridge which Germany was seeking to obtain when the *Bismarck* sank the *Hood* off the coast of Greenland. The southern bridge extends by way of Morocco and Dakar through the Azores and Cape Verde Islands across the Atlantic to Brazil. The Nazis have, as we know, already penetrated into Morocco and West

Africa. In Latin America, they have long plied their treacherous trade.

The day I spoke in New York, the Vice-President of the United States, Mr. Henry Wallace, who was present, referred to Canadians as the Keepers of the northern bridge. That is a striking description of Canada's task as it has been performed, now, for almost two years, in relation to this hemisphere.

We Canadians have indeed been the Keepers of the northern bridge which leads not only from Norway to North America but, also, from Canada and the United States to Britain. The existence of this North Atlantic bridge, like the one in the South Atlantic, should be a reminder to all on this continent that, unless the tide of Nazi aggression can be turned back, we shall face inevitably, to-morrow, a battle of hemispheres.

It has been the recognition of all this that has led the President, within the past week, to land armed forces of the United States in Iceland. It was the recognition of this which led the President, some months ago, to have the United States assume protection of Greenland. For the same reason, United States forces are co-operating to-day in Newfoundland with our own defence forces in the protection on land, at sea and in the air of that strategic island. It should be, as I am sure it is, a source of pride to every Canadian that, at the very outbreak of war, Canada assumed a special responsibility for the protection of Newfoundland; also that, for a year, Canadian troops garrisoned Iceland, and while on duty there, vastly strengthened that country's defences. Not only have we guarded the North Atlantic bridge, we have been strengthening its structure, month in and month out ever since the commencement of war.

Nor can we afford to forget, as we look across the Pacific, that, beyond its waters, we also face a continent which, for five years past, has been in arms; and that the most powerful of the warring nations in the East is an axis partner of Nazi Germany. In whatever direction we look out from this western hemisphere, we see a world ravaged by the fires, torn by the destruction, and convulsed by the horrors of warfare. Month by month, the world-encircling danger is closing in upon this continent. That circle must be broken; that menace must be destroyed. If they are not, the whole western hemisphere, to the extent of its entire resources, will inevitably be drawn into the world conflict.

Consequences of a Nazi Triumph in Europe

There are those who say that Hitler would not dare to try to invade this hemisphere. Let us suppose they are right. Suppose Hitler were to go no further: what would be the consequences of a complete Nazi triumph, in Europe alone?

We already see how Nazi Germany is drawing upon the resources of conquered and enslaved territories to increase the industrial might which is the real foundation of her military power. The agricultural resources of France, of the Low Countries, of Denmark, and of Central Europe are already being used for the production of food to supply Nazi needs. To the same end, Hitler seeks to add to his domain the fertile plains of the Russian Ukraine.

On this foundation of adequate food production and with access to the raw materials of Africa and Asia, Germany herself would become the arsenal and workshop of the entire continent of Europe. With her control of all heavy industries, Germany could keep her great military machine at the peak of its power. The defeated nations would be permanently stripped of the means of resistance to their Nazi overlords.

Look next at what the achievement of this great design would mean for the western hemisphere. Without any attempt at the invasion of this continent, Nazi Germany would already have dealt a demoralizing blow at our standards of life. Look for a moment at the effect upon agriculture. Without world markets, there can be no permanent prosperity for our great primary industries. The Nazi preparations for war, the war itself, and the extension of the blockade have already created enormous surpluses of agricultural commodities, like wheat, which we normally export. The control of Europe by Hitler would end all European trade save on Hitler's terms. The destruction of Hitlerism will alone make possible the reopening of the channels of trade, and the restoration of markets for our exportable surpluses.

Not only could there be no permanent prosperity, but there might well be no future at all for western agriculture in a world in which the eastern hemisphere was dominated by Germany and her axis partners. Without markets in the old world, our western plains would face an economic drought beside which the natural droughts, experienced in the past, would pale into insignificance. Whether the rains fell or whether they failed to come, Nazi domination in the old world would make, of western Canada, an economic desert.

A Struggle Between Hemispheres

Agriculture would be the first victim of a Nazi victory, but it would not be the only victim. Unless the new world is able speedily to match and to surpass the industrial strength of Germany, apart altogether from actual invasion, all our energies on this continent, for years to come, will be absorbed in a terrible struggle between hemispheres. We will face a feverish race of armaments of which we shall see no end. We will be forced into totalitarian methods to meet the totalitarian threat. More and more of our resources will be poured into armaments; less and less will be left to maintain our standards of life and civilization. If Hitler is not defeated in the old world, the new world, to maintain its economic existence, and to save itself from actual conquest, will be dragged down to the slave standards which Hitler is imposing on lands he has conquered.

But the possibility of invasion is something that can no longer be ignored. Unless Britain survives, and unless the forces that seek to preserve the freedom of the seas triumph in the battle of the Atlantic, an attempt at invasion of this continent of North America would follow as inevitably as night follows day. Hitler has forced the present generation to recognize that the modern world cannot survive half slave and half free. No one to-day can escape the choice between freedom and slavery. If he fails to choose between freedom, that means he has already chosen slavery.

This is the choice which Canada made in 1939. Seeing the world-encircling danger already on the horizon, as a united people, we went out to meet and combat it. To-day the whole continent has awakened to the danger.

The Canadian people may well be proud that, of all the peoples in the new world, they were the pioneers in resisting Hitler's attempt at world domination. When war came, we did not hesitate to take up the struggle for freedom in the old world, and in all the world. For the second time, in a generation, our country is in the vanguard of freedom.

EXPANSION OF CANADA'S ARMED FORCES

Canada played a large part in the last war. In this war we have a far greater task, and a very different task. Let me recall some of the differences. From 1914 to 1918 our main task was the raising of an army: almost all that Canada asked for was men for the army. On the sea, we depended almost entirely on Britain's navy. Neither had Canada an air force of her own. Canada's industrial effort was comparatively small. Britain produced most of our equipment and supplies. Britain even helped Canada to finance Canada's part in the war.

Let me now give you very briefly the record of expansion of Canada's armed forces in this war. At the outbreak of war, there were less than 10,000 men in the three branches of the permanent armed forces; to-day there are some 300,000 men in Canada's armed forces at sea, on land and in the air. This figure does not include the numbers, about 170,000, enrolled in the reserve army.

In the navy, at the outbreak of war there were some 20 ships and less than 2,000 men; to-day there are 200 ships and 20,000 men.

In the permanent active militia there were, at the outbreak of war 4,000 men; to-day the active army contains over 200,000 men enlisted for service in any part of the world. In addition, the young men called up for training under the National Resources Mobilization Act will be retained under arms for duty in Canada. This will relieve enlisted men for service elsewhere.

When war began, there were 4,000 men in the air force; to-day there are 60,000.

Apart from coastal patrol and convoy duties, ships and men of Canada's navy have been sharing in the defence of the coasts of Britain. Thirteen Royal Canadian Air Force Squadrons are already serving in Britain; many additional Canadian graduates of the Air Training Plan are serving with the Royal Air Force. Thousands more Canadian pilots and airmen will follow them to Britain before the year is out.

The defenders of Britain now include 82,000 of the soldiers in Canada's active army. Very soon, they will number 100,000. The Canadian Corps of two divisions with corps troops and many thousands of re-inforcements, together with specialized units, such as forestry troops, and the tunnelling companies which have been improving the defences of Gibraltar, have been overseas for many months. They have now being joined by an army tank brigade, and detachments of the third infantry division. The rest of the third division and a fourth, an armoured division, are scheduled to go to Britain this year. In addition to the armed forces in Britain, there are Canadian garrisons in the West Indies and, as I have mentioned, in Newfoundland.

Canadian coast defences have been expanded in recent months and a number of new batteries brought into action. Since the outbreak of war, these defences have been substantially strengthened with new armament and equipment. Important harbours have been made proof against submarine and torpedo so that men-of-war and merchant vessels may lie at anchor in security during their brief periods of rest, refit and loading of cargo. Mine-sweepers are constantly at work in the ship channels to ensure freedom from mines. Anti-submarine vessels are continuously on patrol in search of enemy U-boats. Air patrols cover hundreds of miles of our coastal waters in endless reconnaissance flights, ready to report and where possible to attack air, surface, or submerged enemy units. Plans to cover all likely contingencies have been made by the three fighting services who work at all times in the closest co-operation and harmony.

In Newfoundland, Canada has important commitments for the defence of the island and its ports. The protection of Newfoundland waters has been included in the general scheme of defence of our eastern coast. The number of Canadian sailors, soldiers and airmen providing these defences has steadily been augmented, and close co-operation with the United States forces defending the leased areas is maintained in accordance with the plans of the Canada-United States Permanent Joint Board on Defence.

I do not need to tell anyone in western Canada how immense is the programme of air training we have undertaken in this country. The evidence is all around us on these western plains. Air training in Canada to-day, has expanded for beyond the wide limits set in the original Air Training Plan. The greater part of the air training for the whole British Commonwealth is concentrated on Canadian soil.

Expansion of Canada's War Industries

It must never be forgotten that the present war is a war of machines, as well as of men. Canada has every reason for pride in her war production. We are building, indeed, we have already all but built, an aircraft industry from the ground up.

We are developing a large shipbuilding industry. We have already built a large number of corvettes and mine-sweepers for Canada's navy and for Britain's. Canadian corvettes have given Canada a new fame on the sea. We are also building cargo ships, so desperately needed for the present phase of the struggle. In all parts of Canada, our shipyards are humming with the activity of the men who are making the ships for the delivery of goods to Britain. We are sending all the food to Britain that ships can be found to carry.

For months, Canada has turned out motor transport vehicles, by hundreds daily, both for her own forces and for Britain's. Practically all the motor transport used by the British forces in the North African campaign was made in Canada. Canadian factories are making machine-guns, trench mortars, bombs for aircraft, great quantities of shells and ammunition, electrical apparatus and radio equipment. The latest development is the making of field guns; the first of these were turned out at the huge new plant at Sorel, Quebec, on Dominion Day. Before the year ends, Canada will be making naval guns, anti-aircraft and anti-tank guns and infantry rifles.

Universal carriers have been in production for months; both Mark 111 tanks and cruiser tanks are now being delivered from Canadian workshops. The output of steel and of the base metals and other raw materials of war production has been greatly expanded to meet the growing proportion of Canada's war industry. The tremendous expansion of productive activity has absorbed great numbers of men; many thousands more will be needed. From our limited manpower in Canada, we must recruit the men required to make the tools, as well as the men needed to use them.

The Call to Arms

I have already said that no one to-day can escape the choice between freedom and slavery. The choice is not one which comes only to nations and to governments; it is a choice which must also be made by individuals, and by every individual.

Let me repeat, once more, the issue in this war as I see it. It constitutes Canada's "Call to Arms". I give it, not only to the young men, whose services we seek to enlist in our armed forces to-day. I give it to every man, woman and child in Canada. It affects the lives of every one of us.

We believe that everything which free men value and cherish, on this side of the grave, is in peril in this war. The right of men, rich and poor, to be treated as men; the right of men to make the laws by which they shall be governed; the right of men to work where they will, at what they will; the right of womankind to the serenity and sanctity of the home; the right of children to play in safety under peaceful heavens; the right of old men and women to the tranquillity of their sunset; the right to speak the truth in our hearts; the right to worship, in our own way, the God in whom we believe.

Give that ''Call to Arms'' a place in your minds and hearts; post it where all can read it on the bill-boards of our cities and towns; hang it on the walls of your homes; and see how long you will have to wait for the response it will evoke!

> ''It is a calumny on men to say that they are roused to heroic action by ease, hope of pleasure, recompense—sugar plums of any kind, in this world or the next.''

That you will recognize as one of the passionate utterances of Thomas Carlyle.

> ''In the meanest mortal,'' he adds, ''there lies something nobler. . . . It is not to taste sweet things, but to do noble and true things, and vindicate himself under God's heaven, as a God-made man, that the poorest son of Adam dimly longs. Show him the way of doing that, the dullest day drudge kindles into a hero. They wrong man greatly who say he is to be seduced by ease. . . . Kindle the inner genial life of him, you have a flame that burns up all lower considerations.''

How often those words have come into my mind as I have visited the different training centres on my journey across this continent and have looked into the faces of the young men—many of them "raw recruits" —who have done me the honour of permitting me to take their salute.

Never forget that every man in uniform to-day is an upholder of freedom. Never forget that the glory of Canada's fight for freedom in this world struggle is the very significant fact that all she has done, has been done of her own free will. Keep clear the real issue as it is and no compulsion will be needed to find all the men required for the armed forces of Canada overseas. We shall produce a race of happy warriors, the light in whose eyes is the light of liberty, and the fire in whose hearts is the fire of their souls, dedicated to the service of their fellow-men. Here is a wall of defence which no enemy can tear down or destroy. If maintained, it will be the strength of our young nation, in this hour of the world's peril, and its imperishable glory through ages to come.